MUSTANG
THE INSPIRATION

THE PLANE THAT TURNED THE TIDE OF WORLD WAR TWO

PHILIP KAPLAN

Pen & Sword
AVIATION

First published in Great Britain in 2013 by
PEN & SWORD AVIATION
An imprint of
Pen & Sword Books Ltd
47 Church Street
Barnsley
South Yorkshire
S70 2AS

ISBN 978 1 78159 046 1

A CIP catalogue record for this book is
available from the British Library

Pen & Sword B   Sword Aviation,
Pen & Sword Fa   Sword Military,
Pen & Swo   word Atlas,
Pen & Sword Ar   cliffe True Crime,
Wharncliffe Tra   Iilitary Classics,
Leo Cooper,   mber When,

For a complete list of Pen & Sword titles please contact
PEN & SWORD BOOKS LIMITED
47 Church Street, Barnsley, South Yorkshire, S70 2AS, England
E-mail: enquiries@pen-and-sword.co.uk
Website: www.pen-and-sword.co.uk

CONTENTS

INTRODUCTION 7

ENGLAND EXPECTS 9

INSPIRATION 18

COMPARING APPLES AND LEMONS 29

BLAKESLEE'S DEAL 43

ON TO BERLIN 52

HIGH ACHIEVERS 60

STROBELL AND OVERSTREET 75

THREE TURNING, ONE BURNING 84

DOUBLE-BIRD 95

KOREA 110

FOURTH BUT FIRST 119

POSTWAR 128

KEEP 'EM FLYING 136

FLYING MUSTANG 143

WAR STORIES 152

The author is particularly grateful to the following people for their kind, generous assistance in the research, preparation, and development of this book: Malcolm Bates, Tony Bianchi, Robert Cooper, David Forrest, Royal Frey, Adolf Galland, James Goodson, Stephen Grey, Roger Hall, Eric Holloway, Charles Hewitt, Jack Ilfrey, Frank Johnson, Lynn Johnson, Hargi and Neal Kaplan, Brian Kingcome, Walker Mahurin, Eric Marsden, Judy and Rick McCutcheon, Merle Olmsted, Alan Geoffrey Page, Gunther Rall, Ray Wagner, Hubert Zemke.

Grateful acknowledgement to the following for the use of excerpts from their published and unpublished texts: J.G. Ballard, Donald Blakeslee, Benjamin O. Davis, Jr., Alan Deere, John De Vries, James Farmer, James H. Doolittle, Irwin Dregne, Roger Freeman, Don Gentile, Bill Geiger, John Godfrey, James Goodson, Lee Gover, Grover Hall, Jr., William Hess, Thomas Hitchcock, Jack Ilfrey, Kelly Johnson, Walter Konantz, Harvey Mace, Merle Olmsted, William Overstreet, Charles Portal, Edgar Schmued, Robert Strobell, Ray Wagner, Henry C. Woodrum, Chuck Yeager, Hub Zemke.

If it looks right, it will probably fly right—a tired old saying among airmen, but one that persists. Think if you will of the handful of aeroplanes that most people would probably agree are the best-looking examples of all. The list is short but distinguished and the proof is in the enthusiastic common view of most pilots who have flown them—for nearly all, it was love at first sight and first flight. For most that little list includes the Vickers-Supermarine Spitfire (especially the early Marks), the Douglas DC-3, the Hawker Hunter, the Lockheed Constellation, the Concord, and the North American Mustang. Of these, the Spitfire and Mustang stand out and remain extra special to the majority of pilots who have been privileged to fly them. One common thread exists among those who have experienced both of these fine machines; an opinion that seems to hold up even after a lifetime of flying the best the aviation design community has created. "While the Spitfire may have a slight edge in light-touch handling, if I have to go to war in one type, I'll take the Mustang every time." I have heard that sentiment repeatedly and without reservation.

Former transport pilot Len Morgan noted his impressions after his first flight in a Mustang: "The feeling of power and speed and freedom of action was, to one of my previous experience, utterly exhilarating. It was like getting out of a moving van and onto to motorcycle. They would have smiled back at the field had they been able to witness the cautious experiments that followed—mild dives with the airspeed walking up past the 450 mark, zooms that sent the rate-of-climb needle to the peg, vertical turns that ate up a lot of sky and forced the g-meter up past 4 (before it faded out). Man, it was fun! As much fun as learning to fly all over again."

Near the end of 1943, the bold—many called it misguided—American campaign of daylight precision bombing raids on strategic targets in German-occupied Europe was failing on a grand scale. The rate of loss in men and planes had become staggering and unsustainable; the achievements to that point questionable. The U.S. Eighth Army Air Force had been fighting its way to and from targets that were savagely defended by flak gunners on the ground and determined Luftwaffe fighter pilots in the air. The American bomber crews were largely dependent on their own air gunners for their defence; the P-47, P-38, and Spitfire fighters sent up to escort and protect the bombers simply lacked the range to stay with their charges all the way into Germany and back to their English bases. And the bomber crewmen were unable to protect themselves well enough to prevent the slaughter they were facing late in that grim year.

The importance of the so-called Combined Bombing Offensive; the RAF operating by night and the Americans by day, lay in the Allied determination to stop German war production and end Germany's ability to continue the war. By the fall of 1943, however, the loss rate of Eighth Bomber Command had reached a critical point and its commanders were forced to temporarily suspend bombing operations, lick their wounds and regroup. The notion that a large, well-organized bomber force could effectively protect itself in such attacks had been proven wrong. It was obvious that a new, highly capable long-range escort fighter was desperately needed to shepherd the heavy bombers of the Eighth on their lengthy missions, raising their odds of survival to an acceptable level.

That fighter, the North American P-51 Mustang, began arriving in England in small numbers late in 1943. The first ones were allocated to the fledgling 354th Fighter Group, Ninth Air Force, whose combat debut escorting the B-17s and B-24s of the Eighth, took place in December. It was the first sign of a rescue for the daylight bombing effort. By early 1944, Mustangs were filling the inventories of the fighter groups of the Eighth, making possible the large, powerful and sustained attacks its planners in the former girl's school at Wycombe Abbey, Bucks., intended. The show was once again on the road.

In the Mustang, the strategic bombers of the Eighth finally had the plane that could go the distance with them and give them the measure of security they required to survive and prevail. The journey of this great fighter plane begins with an early Second World War requirement of the British for a new fighter more capable than the Spitfire and Hurricane of the time, and the marvelous marriage of an American airframe with the Rolls-Royce Merlin aero engine. It considers the competition being built by other American warplane makers and looks at the arrival in England of the first Mustang escort fighters. It continues with raids on Germany, experiences of high achieving pilots, the long-range bombing campaigns in both Europe and the Pacific wars, the example of the famous 4th Fighter Group, the Korean War of the 1950s, the postwar activity of the Mustang, the warbird phenomenon, and concludes with a taste of what it was like learning to fly the "Cadillac of the skies", as the young boy in J.G. Ballard's *Empire of the Sun* refers to the liberating Mustang flashing low overhead near his Shanghai prison camp.

ENGLAND EXPECTS

Late in the 1930s it was apparent to many people on both sides of the Atlantic that a new war in Europe was all but inevitable. On September 30th 1938, the British Prime Minister Neville Chamberlain returned to England from a meeting in Munich of the major European powers. Only Czechoslovakia had not been represented. Chamberlain and the others had agreed to permit Germany's leader, Adolf Hitler, to annex the Czech Sudetenland, an area on the Czech-German border inhabited mainly by ethnic Germans. The primary signatories of the agreement, Britain, France, and Italy, had chosen to appease Hitler in the belief that their action would prevent a new war. Hitler had already annexed Austria in March and most western observers thought that he would demand the Sudetenland next.

The nations of western Europe were anxious to avoid another war. Britain and France both perceived Germany as outgunning them and they were struggling to achieve parity. Italy, too, was unready for such a conflict. In a meeting with Hitler on September 22nd, Chamberlain was told that the German army would occupy the Sudetenland by the 28th and, in the hope of avoiding war, the British premier got Hitler to agree to a last-ditch four-power conference over the disputed territory, a meeting that was convened on the 29th and attended by Hitler, Chamberlain, Édouard Daladier of France, and Benito Mussolini of Italy.

Early the next morning a deal was struck that essentially sacrificed Czechoslovakia in return for peace. Britain and France informed the Czechs that if they wanted to resist Germany, they would be on their own, and, seeing the futility of their position, they reluctantly agreed to the annexation and de facto German control of Czechoslovakia. On the 30th, Chamberlain asked Hitler to agree to a peace treaty with

Britain, which the German leader promptly signed. It was that
piece of paper that Neville Chamberlain waved at reporters
later that day when his plane arrived at Heston Aerodrome,
near the London Heathrow airport of today. He beamed pro-
claiming that the paper meant "peace for our time." Winston
Churchill, who would later replace Chamberlain as prime minister, said of the appeasement of Hitler that the prime minister had had a choice between war and dishonor. He chose dishonor and got war.

The British Air Ministry believed that it's Vickers-Supermarine
Spitfire and Hawker Hurricane (both Rolls-Royce Merlin-
engined fighters) could easily meet RAF Fighter Command's
requirement for the defence of Great Britain in the coming
conflict. Air Ministry officials had little interest in any other
fighter types and none in anything then being produced in
the United States. There was simply no match for the speed,
manoeuvrability, and fire power of the Spitfire at the time.
The Spitfire and the Hurricane were, however, defensive
weapons and relatively short on range.

As the European war entered its fifth month, officials in
the British defence establishment finally realized that the
RAF needed a fighter of greater range to meet the threat of
Italy to Egypt and that of the Japanese to Singapore. The Air
Ministry wanted 1,000 new fighters for delivery in 1941. With
poor judgement and little to choose from, they attempted to
order the American Brewster Buffalo, but Brewster could
supply no more than 170 of the planes during 1941 and the
British had to look elsewhere for their aircraft.

By the end of 1939, France was also desperate for new
fighters and purchased 420 H75A Hawks and 259 H81A
fighters (an export version of the P-40) from the American
Curtiss Company. After France fell to the Germans in June
1940, the RAF inherited the Curtiss aircraft that had been

ordered by the French. The British, however, still had a critical fighter need and required more planes than Curtiss alone could provide. Even before the Curtiss fighter production programme had begun, the British were shopping for another source of P-40 production. On February 25th 1940 they had approached North American Aviation in Los Angeles, whose Harvard trainer had served them well since 1938, asking company president J.H. "Dutch" Kindelberger to consider building the Curtiss plane for them.

Kindelberger's chief designer, Edgar Schmued, a forty-year-old talented German design engineer who emigrated to the United States in 1930, had worked for North American since February 1936. He was a quiet, methodical man consumed with the desire to build the best fighter plane in the world, and he was well prepared when Kindelberger dropped by his office one afternoon in early March 1940 to ask: "Ed, do we want to build P-40s here?" "Well, Dutch, don't let us build an obsolete airplane. Let's build a new one. We can design and build a better one."

Kindelberger replied: "I'm going to England in two weeks and I need an inboard profile, a three-view drawing, performance and weight estimates, specifications, and some detail drawings on the gun installations to take with me." He told the designer to make it the fastest plane he could and to build it around a man five feet ten inches tall and weighing 140 pounds. He asked for two 20mm cannon in each wing and that the plane meet all design requirements of the US Army Air Corps. Work on the new fighter began on March 15th and on April 11th Sir Henry Self, director of the Anglo-French Purchasing Commission, signed a letter of intent to buy 400 of the new aircraft. It was agreed that the unit price would be just in excess of $40,000.

Born at the end of December 1899 at Hornbach near the town of Zweibrücken, Germany, Edgar Schmued was the fourth of the six children of the dentist, Heinrich Schmued. Edgar was interested in technical subjects from his early childhood onward. He was, by his own admission, a poor student, but he quickly became fascinated with aviation from age eight and read everything he could find on it, taking full advantage of the local library. His father indulged the interest, buying him every aviation book he wanted that was not available in the library. When he was ready to enter university or technical school, the family was not able to afford the tuition, so Edgar's father bought the textbooks required and the boy became a self-taught aeronautical engineer and aeroplane designer.

Without a formal degree, it was necessary for young Edgar to begin his career as an apprentice in a small factory. "I was a volunteer [apprentice] in an engine factory and my father was able to impress the owner of the factory with the necessity of giving me the best training possible. I was started on the bench and did quite a bit and then I changed over to machines. I was working on a lathe, a milling machine, a shaper, and on a large lathe, and was also learning hand forging. I became quite adept in this art and ultimately the owner gave me a project to build one of his engines completely from scratch. It turned out to be a very nice project, and at the completion of my two years there , I had also completed this engine. I was very, very proud of that. Now I was at least started properly. I was free and I did quite a bit of work at home. I was studying books on all fields, anything technical interested me, particularly aviation.

With Germany and Austria at war in 1917, Edgar was not conscripted as he was already working as a mechanic in the Austro-Hungarian Flying Service. With the German surrender the following year, he returned to his family and began work on his home-built sports biplane to be powered by a three-cylinder Belgian-made Anzani engine. The terms of the Versailles Treaty at the end of the war required the return of any property taken when Germany occupied other countries. Members of the Allied Control Commission learned of Edgar's aeroplane project and confiscated his engine. "This ended my attempt to build an airplane, since I couldn't afford to buy another engine."

Inflation, unemployment, and political instability were threatening the fledgling Weimar Republic in the mid-1920s. Edgar had married and the couple had a son, Rolf. Edgar's two brothers had already emigrated to Brazil and, in 1925, he too went there in search of an aviation career. His family remained in Germany pending his ability to bring them out to join him. There he joined General Motors, Brazil, as head of their field service units and agencies. Most impressed by Edgar's ideas, his field service manager urged him to go to the United States to properly develop and utilize his visions.

Charles Lindbergh's famous trans-Atlantic flight to Paris in 1927 had stimulated a boom in aircraft production. General Motors' Fokker Aircraft Corporation at the Teterboro Airport, New Jersey, was prospering and looking for promising new employees when Edgar arrived there early in 1930. He got a job with Fokker and then immediately enrolled in an English course at the Broadway Evening School for the Foreign Born where, in May 1931, he earned a certificate commending the quality of his work.

The busy assembly line at Fokker was crowded with three-engined F-10 and four-engined F-32 transport planes, despite the huge stock market crash of the previous year. At Fokker, Schmued discovered that American aircraft companies lacked preliminary design departments and he promptly organized the first such department in the United States there at the Teterboro factory. As its head he was positioned to do substantial design work for the company's new models.

By June, General Motors had formed the General Aviation

Corporation, dissolving Fokker Aircraft Corporation of America in the process. All the GAC shares were held by North American Aviation (NAA) and again, Anthony Fokker remained in the mix as chief engineer. NAA also bought controlling interest in the small Berliner-Joyce Aircraft Corporation which was located near Baltimore, Maryland.

One effect of the growing economic depression was a diminishing of transport aircraft construction by April 1931 when a Fokker transport crashed, killing Knute Rockne, the revered football coach of Notre Dame University. The subsequent publicity ended sales for Fokker. The company's fortunes declined, Anthony Fokker resigned, and the plant closed. The remaining General Aviation operations were then relocated to a factory at Dundalk, Maryland, near the Berliner-Joyce Baltimore plant.

Ed Schmued, his wife and son, moved to Dundalk where, in April 1931, he was appointed project engineer for the General Aviation YO-27 three-place observation plane for the U.S. Army. In this environment, Ed learned a lot about project administration, but the continuing depression spelled the end for the Dundalk plant and the jobs of 1,100 of the 1,300 employees. In January 1935 what had been General Aviation was now North American Aviation, with Dutch Kindelberger at the helm, Lee Atwood as his number two. Their first important project was the NAA entry in the Army basic trainer competition, the NA-16. The completed prototype was rolled out on April 5th and and delivered to the Army at Wright Field, Ohio, for fly-off testing against Seversky's rival BT-8. The North American entry won the day and the contract. A $25 prize went to Ed Schmued for his design of a new company logo, a flying eagle on a triangle background, which was applied to the rudder of the NA-16.

Kindelberger believed that North American's future lay in sunny southern California where the good flying weather, lower real estate costs, expanding economy, and the opportunity to have a new, custom-built factory were waiting for him. He had worked for Donald Douglas in Santa Monica and had seen Reuben Fleet move Consolidated Aircraft west to San Diego. With the approved Army contract for the first batch of BT-9s (the NA-16 basic trainer) in hand, Kindelberger signed a lease commiting to pay $600 a year for a 20-acre site on the east side of Mines Field in Inglewood near Los Angeles. Work soon began on the new NAA plant and the Los Angeles area became home to the workers of North American who, together with those of the other area aircraft makers, would contribute to doubling the L.A. population within a few years.

Though ready to go west with Kindelberger and the rest of the NAA staff, Ed Schmued was persuaded by his wife Luisa to remain on the U.S. east coast, and take a position with the aeroplane maker Bellanca at New Castle, Delaware. While there he qualified for U.S. citizenship, receiving it in October 1935. His unhappyness with the policies and procedures at Bellanca was obvious to Luisa who soon relented, and the Schmued family left by car for California to join the NAA team in Inglewood.

As they neared the end of their journey, tragedy struck when their car was hit head-on by that of an elderly Kansas couple. Luisa was killed, their teenage son Rolf had only cuts and bruises, and Ed suffered a badly broken leg, a concussion and an eye injury. He lay in the Coachella Valley Hospital until January 1936. In February he was finally able to start work at North American and in so doing, to immerse himself in demands of his job to fully occupy his mind helping him to recover emotionally from the loss of his wife.

Two comments from that era describe the company that Ed Schmued would serve faithfully for the rest of his life. Charles Lindbergh: ". . . a very efficient establishment—in many ways the most efficient I have yet seen. Inspection of the huge plant reveals straightforward working. There are no tangents, no missteps. From the 200 men working in the drafting room on the second floor . . . to the new planes ready for delivery, there is no wasted motion. Under the saw- toothed skylights a double assembly line works and raw material at the starting end takes on new additions every few minutes as the plane is built in a manner that reminds one of a striptease dancer in reverse."

James H. Kindelberger: "My one thought is to sell enough of our products to keep the organization going without any layoffs. There are a lot of these men to whom a layoff is little short of a tragedy. They are raising families and need every dollar they can make. I just hope to be able to keep them constantly employed and earning, for that's what makes good American citizens." Schmued: "Dutch brought new initiative and vigor to the organization. He was very inspiring and spent a good deal of time with me on new ideas."

The successful development of the BT-9 led in June 1938 to a contract from Britain for 200 examples of the marvelous new trainer the RAF called the Harvard. The plane would ultimately become an all-metal airframe, a company standard established during the project. The U.S. Army Air Corps would call it the AT-6 Texan, to the U.S. Navy it was the SNJ.

In July 1939, Ed was part of the team that designed the NAA entry for the Army's medium bomber competition, the aeroplane that would become the B-25 Mitchell. Designated NA-62, the North American proposal triumphed and the company received a contract for 184 of the new planes. Schmued's contribution to the design effort included the preliminary design, the bomb racks and rack controls and he devoted some of his time to developing ideas for fighter designs that might one day be useful to the company. The B-25 would become the most important American medium bomber of the Second World War.

By the end of the year, the company had an additional 600 Harvards in the order book, 230 more trainers for France, and 251 BT-14s for the Army. At that point it had a backlog of orders worth more than fifty million dollars and employed a staff of more than 4,600 people.

INSPIRATION

"The P-51 Mustang became the decisive weapon in the air war, defeating the enemy fighters deep within their own territory. Many factors were involved in winning the war against the Axis in Europe, but few were as important as the North American P-51 fighter." – Ray Wagner, author of *Mustang Designer*

Ed Schmued merged his earlier fighter concepts with a new laminar-flow airfoil to shape the NA-73, as the new plane was designated, and final British approval was given for the purchase of 320 of the planes in that Battle of Britain summer. He spread the design assignment among several of his specialized groups, estimating that one hundred days would be needed to build the first experimental example. The British had required North American to have the plane flight-tested, de-bugged, and in full production within one year, but around the company, serious concerns were surfacing about the new wing and how it might perform. Exhaustive testing, though, soon proved its viability. Schmued's brilliant scheduling and co-ordination resulted in completion of the first aeroplane by both Engineering and the factory shop in only 102 days, almost exactly as promised.

Forty-four years later, Ed Schmued reflected: "We could never build another plane today in a hundred days as we did then. Today, they just don't have what it takes. There are too many levels of authority within the [aircraft] companies. We had formed an exception group of engineers with an enthusiasm that was unequalled anywhere. We worked every day until midnight. On Sundays we quit at six p.m., so we knew we had a 'weekend.' "

The NA-73 was a sleek all-metal, stressed-skin airframe,

designed to be simple and relatively inexpensive to manu-facture. The laminar-flow airfoil produced less drag at high speeds than more conventional airfoils, but also less lift at low speeds, requiring the plane to have larger flaps to keep the landing speed from being too high. The wing had two straight spars and the main landing gear member's track was nearly twelve feet, making landing easier and safer than in the British Spitfire, for example. All three wheels were fully retractable and the tail wheel was steerable and linked to the rudder. The customer had specified the use of a liquid-cooled inline engine and the Allison V-1710 was the only suitable American-built aero engine available. It was slightly larger than the Rolls-Royce Merlin, a bit lighter, and of sim-ilar power at low altitudes. At higher altitudes, however, it could not deliver power like that of the Merlin. The fuel was stored in two self-sealing tanks inboard in the wings. Their combined capacity was 180 U.S. gallons, nearly twice that of the Spitfire.

For armament, the British were requiring two 0.5-inch Browning machine guns in the underside of the nose, syn-chronized to fire through the propeller arc; two 0.5-inch guns in the wings mounted outboard of the landing gear; and four 0.3-inch guns mounted further outboard on the wings.

North American Aviation had originally been created as a holding company in December 1928. It held interests in sev-eral aircraft companies that included Wright Aeronautical, Keystone Aircraft, Travel Air, and the Curtiss aviation com-panies. The car maker General Motors bought a large inter-est in North American Aviation in 1933, as well as acquiring General Aviation Corporation. In 1929 it had purchased the controlling interest in Fokker Aircraft Corporation, whose founder, the famed World War One aircraft designer Anthony Fokker, remained as chief engineer.

In 1934, James H. Kindelberger left the employe of Douglas Aircraft where he had served as chief engineer, to head the new North American Aviation, Inc. He brought his long-time friend Leland "Lee" Atwood with him as vice-president to their new factory near Mines Field (now a part of Los Angeles International Airport), Inglewood, California. Kindelberger, too, foresaw the coming war and was familiar with the characteristics and capabilities of the various aircraft likely to be involved when hostilities began. With the opening rounds of the war in Europe, he got hold of RAF combat reports and used them to help develop ideas for new fighter aircraft.

In World War Two, Americans of German birth were often regarded with suspicion by government security officers and, on one occasion, they entered Ed Schmued's home when he was at work, to look for evidence of Nazi sympathies. His fellow engineers assured them of Ed's uncompromising commitment to Allied victory and Dutch Kindelberger insisted that Ed and his fellow immigrants were essential to the company's war effort. Kindelberger had no doubts about their loyalty. Fortunately, German-Americans in California escaped the terrible mass removal and incarceration that befell Japanese-Americans, and were allowed to make their contribution to the Axis defeat.

Unfortunately for the new North American fighter project, the Allison aero engine factory at Indianapolis failed to deliver the power plant for the test aeroplane on time. It would be a further eighteen days before the engine arrived in Los Angeles for test-fitting in the airframe. The delay resulted because the engine was "government-supplied equipment" provided on an "as available" basis. As the NA-73 was, at that point, a private venture, its priority level was far lower than that, for example, of the P-40, another user of the Allison V-1710. Initial engine run tests were conducted on October 11th, followed by the maiden flight of the NA-73X took place on October 26th with veteran test pilot Vance Breese at the controls. While the engine was the same as that powering the Curtiss P-40, Breese found the NA-73X to be 25 mph faster than the P-40.

Flight testing continued until November 20th when the NA test pilot Paul Balfour neglected to switch the fuel valve to 'reserve' and ran out of fuel fifteen minutes into a test flight. He was forced to put the precious prototype down on a freshly ploughed field where the wheels dug into the soft ground, causing the plane to flip over onto its back. The pilot was not injured, but the aircraft was badly damaged and required a time-consuming rebuild. Ed Schmued acted swiftly to have the second NA-73 (on the shop floor and scheduled to be the first production aeroplane) prepared for flight test so as not to delay the critical test data gathering.

Even before that first flight of the prototype, the British ordered an additional 300 of the new fighters, for a total buy of 620. In the first recorded reference to the fighter by its nickname, the British purchasing authority called it Mustang in a letter to North American on December 9th.

The U.S. Army Air Corps had the right to block any foreign aircraft sales if it regarded them as not in the Army's interest. It allowed the sale on the basis that two early examples of the NA-73 be provided to the Army for its own testing and evaluation. It designated these planes as XP-51.

In 1941, RAF Squadron Leader Michael Crossley, who had destroyed nine German planes while flying Hawker Hurricanes in the Battle of Britain, arrived in California to conduct the British acceptance flight tests on the Mustang I, as the RAF now called it. Ed Schmued recalled: "He was a very pleasant Britisher, six feet two inches tall, but the cockpit was designed for a five foot ten inch pilot. When he sat in the Mustang his knees were just about under his chin, but he didn't complain. After he made his routine flights, which were most satisfactory, he had one more test to do: firing the guns out over the Pacific Ocean. Such gun firing had to have Coast Guard permission, which was a few weeks in coming. The impatient officer said to me: 'I don't understand you Americans; we in England just fire into the countryside and you would be surprised how few people get killed.' "

By July 1942, all 620 aircraft of the British order were completed, delivered and in service with the Royal Air Force. They were used primarily for photo reconnaissance and low-level cross-Channel sweeps in which they shot up German trains, barges and troop concentrations. Of the Mustangs shipped to England, twelve were lost when the *Ocean Venture*, a new, California-built British ship, was torpedoed by a German U-boat on February 8th 1942. Eight more Mustangs went down on another freighter that same week.

The first RAF Mustang I destined for delivery in Britain arrived at Liverpool on October 24th 1941. It had been accepted by the RAF in September and arrived without a radio, gunsight, and other equipment that the British intended to provide from their own manufacturers. When that was done the plane went first to Boscombe Down for evaluation by the Aeroplane & Armament Experimental Establishment and then to Duxford for further evaluation by the Air Fighting Development Unit. The Mustangs delivered to the RAF under the original order were equipped with an F-24 camera installation located behind the pilot's head armour. A second camera for high altitude vertical photography was added later ahead of the tail wheel well.

RAF pilots liked the Mustang and thought it easily the best

American fighter. It was faster than the Mk Vb Spitfire up to 25,000 feet and had twice its range, but the Spitfire could go much higher and had better rates of climb and turn, as well as a much better engine in the Rolls-Royce designed Merlin. British tests of a fully-loaded Mustang resulted in a 370 mph top speed at 15,000 feet, a 30,000-foot service ceiling, and a 990-mile range at a cruising speed of 180 mph. Schmued: "A man in the Air Ministry later confessed to me that he had taken our performance guarantee of 370 mph and knocked it down to 300 mph because he supposed that all American plane manufacturers lied about performance. When he found out our quotation was correct, it opened up new possibilities for our plane."

But the Mustang's performance rapidly eroded at altitudes above 15,000 feet; its Allison engine being supercharged for best performance at low altitudes. It took the Mustang eleven minutes to climb to 20,000 feet while the Spitfire V could get there in seven. The Spitfire and Germany's Messerschmitt Bf 109 were both more agile than the Mustang at higher altitudes, and the Mustang weighed roughly a third more than the Spitfire.

The RAF elected to operate the Mustang I in low-level tactical reconnaissance and ground attack roles to take advantage of the plane's good performance in those situations. It began flying Mustang Is from Gatwick, which is now another major London airport, with the No 26 Squadron in February 1942, and had ten more Mustang squadrons operational by June. Most of them went to work for the Army Cooperation Command replacing the Westland Lysanders and the Curtiss Tomahawks. The first reported aerial victory by the Mustang came when Royal Canadian Air Force volunteer Flying Officer Hollis Hills shot down a Focke Wulf Fw 190 in combat above the British Dieppe commando landings of August 19th 1942. Mustang I performance on combat operations was praised. Its long range, ability to absorb battle damage, and its heavy armament were greatly appreciated in its squadrons as it found and destroyed hundreds of locomotives, barges, and the enemy aircraft on the ground while incurring only a handful of losses in its first eighteen months of operation in Europe.

As a part of the new Lend/Lease Act passed by the U.S. Congress on March 11th 1941, the government was permitted to "lend" American-build aircraft to nations seen as "vital to the security of the United States." In September the U.S. Army Air Corps ordered 150 Mustangs under Lend/lease for delivery to Britain. The prior British orders for Mustangs had all been direct purchases. These Mustang Ias were equipped with four wing-mounted Hispano cannon. Following the Japanese attack on Pearl Harbor, Hawaii, in December, the army repossessed many of these cannon-equipped Mustangs.

Testing of the two NA-73 (redesignated XP-51 by the U.S. Army) examples at Wright Field in Ohio went slowly. The type lacked the priority given to the Army's more favoured fighter test programmes, the Republic P-47 Thunderbolt, Bell P-39 Airacobra, and the Lockheed P-38 Lightning also being conducted at Wright. As testing finally progressed, however, the Army pilots wrote positive reports on the plane, but the service issued no orders for its purchase. After a time, the Senate Special Committee to Investigate the National Defense Program, chaired by Missouri senator Harry S. Truman, who would become president of the United States on the death of Franklin D. Roosevelt in April 1945, looked into the matter. It wondered why the Army was reluctant to order the highly regarded North American plane. One theory of the time held that NAA's Dutch Kindelberger had received demands for bribes in return for a U.S. Army contract and had refused all such demands.

Finally, after the Pearl Harbor attack brought America into

the war, the USAAF Chief of Staff General Henry H. Arnold intervened and by April the Army had ordered 500 NA-97 Mustangs for the ground attack role which were redesignated A-36A. This version was to have hydraulic perforated dive brakes meant to keep diving speeds down to 250 mph. The A-36 is remembered as a pretty good dive bomber with the ability to quietly approach a target and strike almost before the enemy was aware of its presence. The plane could start an attack from 10,000 to 12,000 feet, drop its bombs at 3,000 feet and pull out at about 1,500 feet. It handled well and was easily manoeuvrable at treetop level, and it could cope well with battle damage and still bring its pilot home. While not planned as a fighter, the NA A-36 experienced air combat on many occasions and claims for 101 enemy aircraft destroyed in the air were registered by its pilots. A total of 177 A-36s were lost to enemy action.

In April 1942 Rolls-Royce test pilot Ronnie Harker was invited by the RAF to fly the Mustang I up at Duxford near Cambridge. Harker was impressed by the handling and the fuel capacity of the American fighter, as well as the positioning of the guns in the wing, and he reported favourably to the RAF Air Fighting Development Unit on the general performance of the plane. In his report he suggested that a really special fighter might result if this exceptional airframe were to be combined with the well-proven and fuel-efficient R-R Merlin engine. But the report, and his subsequent lobbying of Rolls-Royce officials and key Air Ministry figures, met with little enthusiasm. Very few of them wanted anything to do with an American-built aircraft.

Nonetheless, Harker persisted and was eventually able to convince senior people at the engine maker that his idea of mating the Merlin with the Mustang was not only likely to produce an amazing new weapon against the Nazis, but would also result in a great deal of new engine business for Rolls. R-R then persuaded the RAF to provide three Mustangs for Merlin installation at their Hucknall factory. There followed a series of modifications and minor redesigns which ultimately led to the Merlin 65-powered Mustang Mk X, the highly successful realization of Harker's inspiration.

Rolls-Royce sent its performance and installation data on the Mk X to North American's design staff who quickly incorporated the Merlin into production Mustangs.

Thomas 'Tommy' Hitchcock, Jr., was the son of an American Racing Hall of Fame horse trainer who had captained the U.S. team in the 1886 inaugural International Polo Cup. Tommy, Jr. joined the Lafayette Flying Corps in France during the First World War. He was shot down and captured by the Germans, but he soon escaped, hid in woods and walked more than 100 miles over eight nights miserable to safety in Switzerland. After the war, he returned to his studies at Harvard, resuming his own polo career and leading the U.S. team to victory in the 1921 International Cup. The energetic, colourful young man for two of F. Scott Fitzgerald's characters in *Tender Is the Night* and *The Great Gatsby*. He returned to the air corps in the Second World War as a Lieutenant Colonel and an assistant air attache at the U.S. Embassy in London. In that capacity Hitchcock flew an early Mustang and, like Harker, enthusiastically urged the further development of the aircraft by cross-breeding it with the Rolls-Royce Merlin 61 engine. It was a recommendation that strongly influenced air force head General Arnold.

In Michigan, Henry Ford was asked to build more Merlin V-12 engines. He declined and agreements were then reached with the Packard Motor Car Company and Continental Motors for the mass production in the United States of the R-R Merlin under license from Rolls-Royce to supplement British production of the power plant. Among many changes necessary for the Merlin-Mustang installation was the move to an enormous four-blade eleven-foot two-inch Hamilton Standard Hydromatic propeller. Packard's changes included a new carburettor, an automatic supercharger speed shift, water-alcohol injection for emergency power, a new Delco magneto, and a new centrifugal separator to prevent oil foaming. In its part of a reciprocal interchange of information, Packard sent 9,000 drawings to Rolls-Royce during the balance of the war.

Convinced of the promise in the rapidly developing Mustang, General Arnold ordered 2,200 of the Merlin-powered fighters for the U.S. Army Air Force in November 1942. America had been at war with Japan, Germany and Italy since the previous December and North American Aviation was inundated with orders for the AT-6 Texan/Harvard trainer, the B-25 medium bomber, and the Mustang. The company expanded its manufacturing facilities at Inglewood and built new plants in Texas and Oklahoma for Mustang production.

Performance testing of the Merlin-engined Mustangs proved the brilliance of Ronnie Harker's idea. The fabulous fighter had a top speed of 441 mph, more than 50 mph faster than the Allison-powered Mustang, with greatly improved performance in virtually all other categories as well.

And by late December 1943, the RAF Air Fighting Development Unit had tested the new, improved P-51B Mustang and was impressed. They described it as: ". . . delightfully easy to handle . . . a much cleaner aircraft than the Spitfire Mk IX and twenty to thirty mph faster at all heights, with a range between fifty to seventy-five percent better. Because of its higher wing loading, the Mustang did not climb or turn as quickly as the Spitfire." When they compared it to a captured Messerschmitt Bf 109G: "The Mustang as faster at all heights and greatly superior in turns . . . while climbing, slightly better above 25,000 feet and worse below 10,000 feet." All things considered, it was the long-range fighter they had been waiting for.

COMPARING APPLES WITH LEMONS

"Let's fight till six, and then have dinner", said Tweedledum.

Between August and December 1941, two XP-51 Mustang examples had been delivered to the U.S. Army for evaluation at Wright Field, Ohio. Both aircraft were equipped with the Allison V-1710 engine and armed with eight .50-caliber and two .30-caliber machine guns. Both had a 170-gallon fuel capacity yielding a range of 750 miles at a 325 mph cruising speed. The manufacturer guaranteed top speed of 375 mph would be exceeded in the testing.

On October 21st North American test pilot Bob Chilton arrived at Wright Field to fly examples of the Spitfire V and Hurricane II to compare their performance and flight characteristics with those of the Mustang. He immediately noticed that the XP-51s had only one flight hour in their logbooks and learned that, as the '51s were not under an Army production contract, they were not considered as important as the other fighter aircraft then at Wright for testing and evaluation, the Republic P-47 and the Curtiss P-60, both scheduled for production in 1942. In fact, when the Army Air Force Pursuit Board met in October of that year to debate the futures of eight production and eighteen experimental pursuit aircraft, the XP-51 was not even among the planes considered.

The Army focused on a wide range of fighter aircraft concepts, advancing several of them to various stages of preliminary development. These included the twin-boomed Vultee XP-54, promoted as a 510 mph sensation; the swept- wing, canard-equipped Curtiss-Wright XP-55; and the strange and tailless Northrop XP-56. Experimental prototypes also were ordered for the Curtiss-Wright P-60, P-62, and the huge XP-71. Work progressed on the XP-39E, the XP-59, and the XP-

63 of Bell Aircraft, Republic's XP-47E and XP-69, while Lockheed concentrated on their XP-49 and XP-58 twin-engined aircraft, and McDonnell on their XP-67. Little wonder there was no room on the table for North American's P-51. Of all the aircraft discussed by the Army Pursuit Board that October, only the Northrop P-61 Black Widow night fighter would ever see combat.

Crucially for Army planners, they had only two pursuit/fighter types then in quantity production for the service, the Bell P-39D Airacobra and the Curtiss-Wright P-40E Warhawk, neither of which was capable of the kind of performance they needed. Their best hope for a successful high-altitude air-superiority fighter lay in the twin-engined, turbo-supercharged Lockheed P-38 Lightning and the Republic P-47 Thunderbolt, should one or both live up to their touted capabilities.

By December 1941, when naval and air forces of the Japanese Empire had attacked the battleships of the U.S. Pacific Fleet at Pearl Harbor, Hawaii, a new urgency prevailed among those Army planners. The best available fighter aircraft were suddenly essential to the rapidly growing American war requirement. The Americans then began to commandeer Lightnings and Airacobras destined for shipment abroad, for their own use, while the flow of Kittyhawks (the export version of the P-40E) and Mustangs to Britain continued unabated.

Testing of the XP-51, meanwhile, was producing some fascinating information that even the previously disinterested U.S. Army Air Corps could not afford to ignore. NACA test pilots found that the plane's laminar flow airfoil was extremely efficient "reducing peak airflow velocities over the wing; postponing and minimizing the 'compressibility effects' then troubling the other fighters of the time. Motion picture photography was used to show the effects of increasing dive speed on the aircraft and test-pilot safety was improved in the course of the flight-test programme. The results of roll rate and dive recovery tests were impressive and the Army soon expressed genuine interest in the Mustang, in the belief that it now had a priority need for "a suitable dive-bomber, low-altitude attack fighter". It asked North American to create a dive-bomber to be designated A-36 from the Mustang.

A contract was issued to the planemaker for 500 A-36As, to be equipped with external racks capable of carrying a 500-pound bomb or 75-gallon drop tank under each wing, and acceleration-limiting dive brakes. By May 1942, Bob Chilton was flight-testing the new dive brakes and by July he was flying dive-bombing tests. In the same period, he had been flying drag tests of the cannon-equipped lend-lease P-51 for the British. Intrigued, the Army planners now found a pressing need for some of these planes for use in tactical reconnaissance squadrons, and requisitioned the first twenty such aircraft to emerge from the factory in July.

Of the 150 Mustangs in that production batch, 93 went to the Royal Air Force, two were retained by North American for engine experimentation, and the final 35 also went to the Army Air Force. 54 of the Army Mustangs were ultimately modified for photo-reconnaissance and re-designated F-6A. Army Air Force interest in the Mustang was increasing and North American executives decided to develop a pure fighter version of the aeroplane; with an improved engine, all .50-caliber armament, and drop tanks for considerably greater range. This was the NA-99 project, which would lead to a USAAF contract for 1,200 P-51As in August 1942.

Most pilots found the Lockheed P-38 Lightning more difficult to fly than the best single-engined fighters of the day. In northern climates the cockpit could be miserably cold and, in such conditions, the twin supercharged Allison engines were especially temperamental, causing constant problems for the pilots and mechanics of the U.S. Eighth Air Force operating from English bases in WWII. It was not until the late appearance of the P-38L model that improved heating, defrosting, and engine fire extinguishing systems became operational. But by then the Eighth had given up on the P-38 as a primary escort fighter for its long-ranging high altitude bombing missions to German-occupied Europe.

The Lightning faired much better in the warmer climate of the Pacific war theatre, where its two-engine performance and over-ocean capability proved particularly useful. Pilots there appreciated the safety of two engines over long stretches of open sea, the plane's great speed, rate of climb, payload, and its nose-mounted concentration of firepower.

The Lightning produced a number of notable fighter aces out there including Major Richard Bong, known as the "ace of aces." Bong finished the war with a total of 40 combat victories and he was a recipient of the Congressional Medal of Honor as well as the Distinguished Service Cross, two Silver Stars, seven Distinguished Flying Crosses and fourteen Air Medals. He admitted that he was actually a poor shot in the air, and had to compensate for his lack of accuracy by getting in dangerously close to the enemy and sometimes flying through the debris of his target aircraft. On one occasion he actually collided with the enemy plane. Bong named his P-38 'Marge' after his fiancé, and carried a large photo of her on the nose of his fighter.

The Lightning proved highly successful for Major Bong, and for the pilots of the 339th Fighter Squadron, 347th Fighter Group, based on the island of Guadalcanal in 1943. On April 14th U.S. Intelligence had learned that Admiral Isoroku Yamamoto, Commander-in-Chief of the Combined Japanese Fleet, was to fly an inspection tour of the Japanese base at Bougainville on April 18th. At the behest of U.S.

President Franklin Delano Roosevelt, a mission was quickly planned to 'get Yamamoto', using eighteen P-38s with long-range fuel tanks to intercept and attack the admiral's plane. The American pilots were briefed that they would be going after "an important high-ranking officer", but were not told who he was. The P-38 pilots flew the 430 miles to the interception point at wave-top height and under radio silence. At 9:34 a.m. they met and engaged Yamamoto's Mitsubishi G4M 'Betty' bomber, a second Betty, and his escort of six A6M Zero fighters. In the encounter, Lt. Rex Barber and Captain Thomas Lanphier each claimed to have downed the bomber carrying Yamamoto, and both were given a half credit for the victory. The action raised morale in the United States and shocked the Japanese.

Of all the fighter planes of the Second World War era, the Lockheed Lightning is certainly among the most fascinating and unusual. In 1937 Clarence Kelly Johnson, the brains behind the Lockheed creative group later called 'The Skunk Works,' began the design of the P-38. It was based on a U.S. Army specification calling for an interceptor able to climb to 20,000 feet in six minutes, no small feat in the late 1930s. Johnson's design group would also create many famous and extraordinarily capable aircraft, including the SR-71 Blackbird spy plane with Mach 3.2 speed and an 85,000-foot service ceiling. But it was the P-38 that sparked his remarkable career and began his reputation as an innovative pioneer in aviation design.

Employing a twin-boom airframe to accommodate two V-1710 12-cylinder Allison engines, Johnson set out to build a fighter unlike anything the Army might have envisioned. He positioned superchargers in the large booms behind the big Allisons to give the plane the required high-altitude performance. He armed it with four .50-caliber machine guns patterned around a cannon in the nose. He gave it a tricycle landing gear, greatly improving the pilot's forward visibility on the ground. And, in the lovely art deco style of the time, he shaped the Lightning in a streamlined elegance in respect of the aviation adage, if it looks right it will probably fly right . . . which it did, for the most part. But the Lightning suffered one particularly serious problem known as "compressibility stall", when the flight controls simply locked up during a high-speed dive. With no known way to overcome the condition, the pilot was forced to bail out. In some instances, the problem became so severe that the entire tail structure of the plane disintegrated.

Kelly Johnson: "I broke an ulcer over compressibility on the P-38 because we flew into a speed range where no one had ever been before, and we had difficulty convincing people that it wasn't the funny-looking airplane itself, but a fundamental physical problem. We then found out what happened when the Lightning shed its tail, and we worked during the whole war to get fifteen more knots speed out of the P-38. We saw compressibility as a brick wall for a long time. Then we learned how to get through it."

Unfortunately, compressibility wasn't the only problem the Lightning had. Its most catastrophic defect was what may be called "asymmetric power", where one of its two engines would fail on take-off, causing the aircraft to flip over and crash upside-down into the ground. In time a procedure was devised for a pilot to cope with asymmetric power situations. But if he was going to live he had to be quick and skillful. It required him to immediately reduce power on the running engine, promptly feather the propeller on the dead engine, and then gradually increase power to stabilize the plane in flight. It was this problem, and the bad reputation it spawned for the P-38, that preceded the new fighter into war.

The Lightning went to war in the Pacific in August 1942. P-38s opened their accounts that month by downing two

Kawanishi H6K "Mavis" flying boats. In that same month a USAAF P-38F joined forces with a Curtiss P-40 to destroy a German Air Force Focke-Wulf Fw 200 raider in the Battle of the Atlantic.

German fighter pilots entering combat with P-38s soon discovered the folly of turning into a head-on attack with the Lockheed plane and its super-concentrated firepower. They were startled too by the Lightning's zoom climb capability, but soon found that, as a dogfighter, the American plane was not quite the dangerous foe they had feared, except when flown by an exceptionally gifted pilot.

In 1943 the American Eighth Air Force was using P-38s to shepherd its B-17 and B-24 bombers on their deep pene-tration daylight bombing raids into Europe. The Lightning pilots suffered considerably from the cold on these missions and the P-38s were eventually withdrawn from the escort role. Many of them found a new job in low-altitude reconnaissance work where they proved far more successful.

"Don't give me a P-39 / With an engine that's mounted behind / It'll tumble and roll / And dig a big hole / Don't give me a P-39." That verse by an unknown wartime author, sums up the view of many American pilots who trained on the Bell fighter at Tonopah in the Nevada desert during 1943. Bud Anderson, among the greatest of all the American fighter aces wrote: "The P-39 could be tricky. 'It'll tumble and spin, and soon auger in', as one of our drinking songs aptly put it. It had a reputation for tumbling end over end, which hardly inspired the pilots. I saw one do something of the sort, go end over end out of control. Later, I asked some Bell test pilots about it, and they said they had tried every trick in the book to make the plane tumble, and never could do it. But you had to be careful with it, particularly if you were new to it. Things happened quickly. This wasn't a forgiving friend like the good old AT-6.

"It was a good-looking airplane. If looks counted for anything, it would have been a great airplane. The Russians absolutely loved them, and wound up with most of them. Under 15,000 feet, the P-39, called the Airacobra, was a decent if underpowered performer. But the Airacobra was mincemeat above 15,000 feet, and useless in Western Europe, where virtually all the flying and fighting was at double that altitude . . . but in October of 1942, I was thrilled to be flying it. It was unique, with its engine behind the cockpit, and the propeller drive shaft running between the pilot's legs. It had a trycycle landing gear, unlike anything in our arsenal except the P-38. And the cockpit was more like a car's, with a door instead of a swing-up or sliding canopy, and windows that actually rolled up and down with a crank. You could taxi the thing while resting your elbows on the sill, like cruising the boulevard on a Saturday night."

Was it a tumbler? The experience of 2nd Lt. Harvey Mace, 357th Fighter Group: "It was decided by somebody that a good training exercise would be to have all three squadrons engage in one huge dogfight. We had this big melee going and I was hot on the tail of an opponent when he pulled up into a loop. At the top of the loop, I happened to look to my left just in time to see some poor soul fall into a tumble. I was so distracted laughing that I let my own airspeed fall too low and the P-39 promptly reminded me of my foolishness by snapping into an immediate tumble of my own. The stick jerked out of my hand and all I could do was keep my knees and hands out of the way of the flailing stick until the airplane decided to do something that I could recognize. Finally, the ship stopped tumbling and settled down absolutely straight and level—but with no airspeed showing on the dial. I very carefully took hold of the now quiet stick by two fingers and gently pushed forward to get the nose down. The fact that it responded showed that there had to be some forward motion. I hardly dared breathe as the nose dropped down enough to where the airspeed needle began to creep up the dial. I didn't do a thing more until I could see 200 mph on the dial. Only then did I re-enter the fray."

The Bell P-39 Airacobra was the third entry in the Army fighter competition of 1937. It was certainly an oddity with its mid-fuselage engine positioning, its car door entry, and its 37mm nose-mounted cannon. And it was quite a performer, at least as a prototype. With a top speed of 390 mph, it was also capable of climbing to 20,000 feet in just five minutes, a full minute less than the time required in the Army specification.

Fighter pilots of the RAF inherited a number of P-39s from a French contract when France fell to the Germans in the spring of 1940. The British pilots disliked the plane for the way its performance fell away above 20,000 feet, for its rather short range (only 430 miles on internal tankage, 690 miles with drop tanks), and most worryingly, for its tendency to spin and the difficulty in recovering from the condition. The RAF realized that it desperately needed a truly effective high-altitude fighter and quickly abandoned the Airacobra.

American pilots in the Pacific were also unhappy with the unconventional Bell fighter, having the same objections as the British, and finding that they simply could not turn or maneuver with the far more agile Japanese Zero. And the 37mm cannon armament of the Airacobra proved ineffective against the Japanese fighter due to the slow rate of fire of the big weapon and the drooping trajectory of the shells. Many P-39 pilots there hated the plane and requested transfers to P-38 units.

Soviet pilots, on the other hand, were enthusiastic in their praise for the Airacobra. Once they got beyond early problems with the radios and with the aeroplane's tendency to spin, they liked the low-altitude speed, the strength of the airframe, and the armament which evidently performed well for them. At most medium altitudes over Soviet territory, these fliers achieved significant results against early Bf-109s and Ju-87 Stukas. Five of the ten highest scoring Soviet aces were P-39 pilots. Nearly half of all the P-39s produced were sent to the USSR. The Soviets managed to successfully utilize this aircraft while, for the most part, the Western Allies could not.

When the Anglo-French Purchasing Commission approached North American Aviation, Los Angeles, in February 1940, their aim was to get the planemaker to build Curtiss P-40s for them to use against the Germans in a war the Americans were then only reading about. In the competition that developed around that 1937 U.S. Army specification for a new fighter, Lockheed, Curtiss, and Bell all produced new designs for the plane they believed would be dominant in the next war. The Curtiss entry was the P-40 Warhawk, a 362-mph Allison V-1710-powerered aeroplane with an 850-mile range and an armament of six .50-caliber wing-mounted machine guns.

The rap against the Warhawk was that it was too slow. In fact, its speed matched that of the Spitfire Mk 1a and the Messerschmitt Bf-109E, and surpassed that of the Hawker Hurricane and the Mitsubishi A6M-2 Zero. Also, it was, for its time, a relatively good, competitive machine. And the conservative Army planners wanted a traditional, proven design; not something as radical as the twin-engined P-38 Lightning which, incidentally, was far more complex and more difficult to build than the P-40. Critics of the Warhawk also knocked it for not being as maneuvrable and nimble in combat as the Zero. The Japanese pilots, however, considered the P-40 their most difficult and dangerous oppponent at low to medium altitudes; they most feared the P-38 at high altitudes and most of them thought the Vought F4U Corsair the best all-round fighter they faced.

The Army chose the P-40 from the others in the competition for a new fighter and awarded a production contract to Curtiss-Wright. By 1940 it was active in British and American squadrons, performing well in most respects and impressing its German adversaries more than the Hurricane had done. P-40s were also quite popular export aircraft, serving in the air forces of the USSR, Canada, New Zealand, Egypt, Brazil, China, and Turkey.

The P-40 is best known for its fighting role with the famous Flying Tigers of U.S. Colonel Claire Chennault. This volunteer group operated in China and Burma from December 1941 through July 4th 1942, destroying 297 Japanese aircraft, with another 153 probably destroyed, in their first six months of combat, against a loss of just twelve of their own planes. Much of their success was due to the superior flying and gunnery skills of the U.S. pilots to that of their opposition. They had to be good, both to prevail and because the P-40 was not without shortcomings, which included an inferior turn rate and rate of climb to those of the Zero.

13,738 P-40s had been built by the end of 1944, when other American fighters, including the P-38, P-47, and the P-51, had replaced the Curtiss plane, ushering in a new standard of fighter performance.

Love it or hate it, you had to be impressed by the sheer size and apparent potential of the Republic P-47 Thunderbolt. Nearly as fast as a Mustang, twice as heavy as a Spitfire, with substantial range, armament and payload, the Jug, as it was known, was a big, high achiever wherever it operated. With 15,677 of the planes built, it was the most heavily produced U.S. fighter aircraft of the war, edging out the Mustang (at 15,386), the P-40 (at 15,000), and the P-38 (at 10,037). The performance envelope of the P-47D Thunderbolt included a top speed of 426 mph at 30,000 feet, a range of 1,800 miles on internal fuel, and an armament of eight .50-caliber machine guns and up to 1,500 pounds of bombs.

The big P-47 entered combat in the European Theatre of Operations early in 1943 with units of the Eighth Air Force where it shouldered much of the escort role for the heavy bombers of the command. Until the advent of the P-51 in sufficient numbers to take over the protection of the heavies, the Jugs performed extremely well. One outfit, the 56th Fighter Group, under the command of Colonel Hub Zemke, accounted for 1,006 enemy aircraft shot down against the loss of just 128 P-47s. Zemke's unit included several of the war's great aces—Francis Gabreski, Robert S. Johnson, Bud Mahurin, and Zemke himself. The rival 4th Fighter Group, commanded by Colonel Don Blakeslee, also flew the Thunderbolt for a while. But Blakeslee didn't like the aeroplane and wasn't shy about expressing his view. When reminded by one his pilots how well the P-47 could dive, Blakeslee remarked: "It ought to dive—it sure as hell can't climb."

What most of its pilots did like about the Thunderbolt was its ability to absorb the punishment of enemy fire and survive to bring them safely back to base. As the missions of the Thunderbolt increased in duration, some changes were made to improve the comfort of pilots. The leg room was increased through the employment of folding rudder pedals, the original seat was replaced by an "armchair" type model, and an automatic pilot was added.

In summing up his opinion of the P-47 relative to the Mustang, one Pacific war pilot recalls appreciating that the Thunderbolt could climb higher, to 40,000 feet, and operate comfortably at that altitude where other aircraft tended to stall out. With its eight machine guns to the Mustang's six, the P-47 had 1/3 more firepower, which he felt made a big difference.

That armament, together with the P-47's ability to carry and deliver 1,500 pounds of bombs (or up to 2,500 pounds when using water-injection for take-off on a long runway) made the Thunderbolt a formidable fighter-bomber. He also considered it a superb strafer and ground-attack weapon against troop concentrations, ships, trains, airfields, ammunition dumps and anti-aircraft installations. For him it was a first-class fighter, having destroyed nearly 12,000 enemy aircraft in the air and on the ground. In performance terms, he has always been impressed by the Thunderbolt's dive capability, believing it could outdive the Mustang and every enemy fighter. But it was the key safety factor in operating the Thunderbolt that caused him to favour the heavy Republic fighter over the Mustang—the size and inherent structural integrity of the Jug airframe. If a pilot had to ditch at sea or belly-land his damaged plane, he was quite convinced that the odds of survival favoured the Thunderbolt pilot over his Mustang counterpart. He saw the "scoop" under the Mustang fuselage as a dangerous impediment to safely ditching or bellying in, should that be necessary.

A further safety consideration relates to the Jug having that big, air-cooled radial engine, rather than a liquid-cooled V-12 like the Mustang. A small-caliber strike to the engine or cooling system of the Mustang, particularly on an over-ocean mission, virtually guaranteed you were going to get wet before you got home, if you got home. And that big Thunderbolt radial engine could take substantial punishment from enemy fire and often keep running well enough to get the pilot back to base. He liked the added comfort and roominess of the larger P-47 cockpit and really appreciated it on the very long seven and eight-hour missions he sometimes had to fly. As for ease in flying, he called attention to the very wide, strong landing gear of the P-47. "When you set it down, it was down," an important consideration on some of the rough, damp and irregular airstrips he had to use.

By the end of 1943, the vastly improved Mustang in the form of the P-51B was in production and on the way to building its reputation in the European air war. The job of these Eighth Air Force P-51s was to escort their 'Big Friend' heavy bombers on high-altitude raids deep into Germany. The other best American long-range escort fighter, the P-47D, was limited to a 400-mile combat radius even with a 108-gallon drop tank and normally had to abandon its charges before the bombers even reached the point where they most needed protection from enemy fighters. Without such protection on a truly effective scale the Eighth was being forced to pull back from its daylight precision bombing campaign, as it could not sustain the level of losses it was incurring.

Along with Rolls-Royce test pilot Ronnie Harker's brilliant inspiration to marry the Merlin engine with the Mustang airframe, had come a similar and equally influential recommendation from American Air Force Major Thomas Hitchcock "to develop the Mustang, one of the best, if not the best airframe that has been developed in the war, as a high-altitude fighter by cross-breeding it with the Merlin 61 engine."

Tommy Hitchcock, who was an assistant air attaché at the American embassy in London, added: ". . . while the prospect of an English engine in an American airframe may appeal . . . to those individuals who are interested in furthering Anglo-American relationships . . . it does not fully satisfy important people on both sides of the Atlantic who seem more interested in pointing with pride to the development of a 100-percent national product, then they are concerned with the very difficult problem of developing a fighter plane that will be superior to anything the Germans have." Fortunately, USAAC General Henry Arnold agreed with Harker and Hitchcock's assessments and was able to report to President Roosevelt in November 1942 that more than 2,200 Mustangs had just been ordered for his service.

BLAKESLEE'S DEAL

By late 1943 the fighter pilots of the American Eighth Air Force in England had heard all the rumours about the new plane the British called Mustang, and the men of the 4th Fighter Group at Debden in Essex were especially eager to get their hands on Mustangs. For some time they had been flying P-47s and were far from pleased with them. Although later models of the Thunderbolt were considerably improved, the planes then being operated from Debden were, in their opinion, "lumbering, over-rated crates that wouldn't climb, wouldn't turn, and whose cockpit had a way of gathering smoke from burning oil, often unnerving the pilot."

But the fighter groups of the Eighth were slow to receive the new machines from North American and as the year wore on, some even tried lobbying General Arnold to equip their outfit at the earliest possible moment. They soon learned that the Ninth Air Force had a higher priority and would be getting their Mustangs ahead of the Eighth's groups.

In this period the 4th was engaged in a friendly rivalry with a sister organization, Hub Zemke's 56th Fighter Group based at Halesworth in Suffolk. Zemke's boys were getting on with the job in their massive Thunderbolts, racking up significant combat scores of ten to fifteen aerial victories a mission and easily outshining the achievements of Colonel Don Blakeslee's boys at Debden. It almost seemed that the 4th Fighter Group pilots were feeling a bit sorry for themselves. They missed the lithe, agile little Spitfires they had enjoyed flying before the coming of the brutish Thunderbolt, and knew that the much vaunted Mustang was much like the quick and deadly Spitfire, only more so.

By the time Zemke's boys had destroyed their 300th enemy aircraft, Blakeslee's pilots had barely managed to down 150, and the gentlemen of Debden explained their deficit with a

whole range of excuses: "They just booger off and don't protect the bombers like we do", as well as "They're just getting
a lot of easy-meat twin-engined stuff." Besides, the 56th was
based up at Halesworth, on the coast, giving them an extra
fifteen to twenty minutes hunting time over Germany. There
were gripes and grumbles aplenty, and not all of them from
the pilots.

Crew chiefs and other mechanics shared the displeasure
of their pilots in that atmosphere of under-achievement. They
all resented it when the first of the new armour-piercing
incendiary ammunition went to the 56th, Zemke's Wolfpack,
as it had become known. But Blakeslee's reaction was different: "No, they've been doing the fighting lately, they rate 'em.
Just wait!"

"It's the ship" became Blakeslee's catch phrase. He had
been selected to mentor the fledgling 354th Fighter Group
through their first few missions shortly after their arrival in
England. He was a great leader, especially in the air where
few if any other flying group commanders had the capability
of truly controlling their pilots in aerial combat. Don Blakeslee
could and did. But he preferred to sleep in his own bed at
Debden each night and flew back there after each mission
with the 354th in a borrowed P-51 to watch his own boys
drool as he dazzled them with tales of its amazing performance and promise. They all ached to fly it. "It's the ship", he
said.

With that brief experience of combat in the Mustang under
his belt, Blakeslee was certain that when his own group was
equipped with the new fighter from North American, they
would very quickly earn their own distinction as the premier
fighter group of the Eighth. He appealed to General William
E. Kepner, Commanding General of Eighth Air Force Fighter
Command, to put his boys in Mustangs immediately. But the
general argued that pressing demands of the great air offen-

sive going on meant that no time could be spared on a lengthy change-over from the 4th's Thunderbolts to Mustangs. Days, even weeks, might be needed for practice flying to accustom them to the hot new fighter, and even more time would be required for the ground crews to familiarize themselves with P-51 maintenance procedures for the liquid-cooled Merlin engines of the '51s. Colonel Blakeslee countered that most of his boys had already flown Merlin-engined Spitfires in the RAF before they transferred into the 4th. And they had continued to fly Spitfires at Debden until the conversion to P-47s, so the mechanics were all familiar with the liquid-cooled Merlins. "General, give me those Mustangs and I give you my word— I'll have 'em in combat in twenty-four hours."

In his fine book *The Look of Eagles*, former 4th Fighter Group ace John T. Godfrey wrote: "Rumours had been flying hot and heavy that we were being transferred from P-47s to P-51s. We had heard a lot of talk about this amazing plane. By cutting the fire power to four machine guns and using a new type of carburetor, it was capable of 1,800-mile flights with its two belly tanks. Our P-47s had only one belly tank which was slung underneath the fuselage. The 51s had them slung underneath each wing, with two more permanent tanks in the wing and another tank just to the rear of the cockpit."

On February 22nd the rumours were confirmed when a lone P-51 landed and all sixty pilots of the 4th were ordered to fly it in preparation for the change-over. Godfrey thought it a beautiful airplane. With its big in-line engine, it reminded him of the Spitfire, and, like the Spitfire, it too was glycol-cooled. The pilots of the group queued up to fly the plane, like housewives at a bargain sale. They each had only forty minutes in the air in the Mustang by the morning of the 28th when the group flew to the Steeple Morden base in their P-47s and traded them for P-51s. The new Mustangs had not been fitted with auxiliary fuel tanks, but they were fuelled and the machine guns were loaded. Their briefing was held on the ground among the planes. Rather than flying back to Debden, Blakeslee led the boys on a fighter sweep to France to familiarize them with the aeroplane the hard way.

Godfrey was sure the Air Force had made no mistake in purchasing the Mustangs from the North American Aviation. He believed they were the hottest planes in the sky. From zero to 30,000 feet they were able to match anything the Luftwaffe put into the air. "If the fighting spirit of the group was high before the advent of the 51s," he thought, "it was now at fever pitch."

But some horrible problems were plaguing the Mustangs— engine trouble, fuel trouble, radio trouble—and worst of all, in addition to their windscreens frosting up, so too did their machine-guns. The guns froze at high altitudes and, in dogfights, they frequently jammed with the force of gravity in a tight turn. That meant straightening out before firing—virtually impossible in the circumstances. Technicians from North American Aviation were rushed to Debden to deal with these problems, but in the interim the great air offensive against Germany was in full swing, and the pilots of the 4th had to fly the '51s, bugs and all.

On March 3rd they flew the first escorted raid on Berlin. In the briefing that morning, the red line from Debden ran off the map and onto the wall. It was a long haul, and the Mustangs were to be the first fighters to go all the way with the bombers to Berlin and back. But the weather turned unfavorable and the bombers turned back. Plagued with Mustang 'bugs,' eight pilots from Godfrey's squadron had to turn back for England. The remaining eight P-51s continue towards Berlin. Separated from the rest of the group, the eight were unable to hear Blakeslee ordering all planes to return to base after he had learned from the bombers the show was canceled.

From the U.S. Army newspaper *Stars and Stripes*: FIVE OF
EIGHT MUSTANGS SURVIVE BATTLE WITH SIXTY
GERMANS A Mustang Base, Mar. 5—The story of an ambush
in which eight Mustang pilots fought their way past sixty
German fighters was told here by the five survivors. Separated
from the rest of their group, the eight Mustang men of the
Eighth AAF were jumped by swarms of enemy fighters which
dived out of the sun in groups of ten and twenty. Maj. Gilbert
O. Halsey, of Chickasha, Okla., gave the order to fight their
way out, and the Mustangs took on the entire Nazi air circus.
Three U.S. pilots were shot down in the melee with FW-190s,
ME-109s, and 210s and even a few Do-217s. Four German
planes were destroyed, two by Capt. Don Gentile, of Piqua,
Ohio,who boosted his total score to ten.

They had flown through a light cloud formation and into
sixty German fighters. Godfrey had no time to count them, but
saw dozens of them above, below, and to their sides; ME-
109s, Me-210s and FW-190s, all looking sinister with their
black crosses glistening as the sun reflected off them. I can't
say they bounced us, for the word is not descriptive enough;
they just poured on us. There was no possibility of flying wing
to another plane. It was every man for himself in the melee of
diving and screaming planes. In the first minutes of flight I
gave no thought to firing my guns; it would have meant flying
straight and level to insure a shot. I was continually turning,
banking, climbing and diving while German planes repeatedly attacked me.

John Godfrey freed himself from the confusion and dived
for the deck. He heard the chatter of some of the other pilots
on the R/T as they tried to re-form. He was relieved to know
that some of them had also escaped and he began climbing to
see if he could spot them. He levelled off at 28,000 feet but
saw no other Mustangs. Calling on the R/T for their positions,
he got no answer. A plane then approached and, because of

its long nose, he thought it was a Mustang. Turning into it he was surprised to find that it was neither a Mustang nor an ME-109, but a new Focke-Wulf; its long nose the latest improvement of the hot German fighter. These new FWs were rumored to have more horsepower than their predecessors, and supposedly capable of giving a Mustang a rough time. We met nearly head-on and both pilots banked hard in preparation for a dogfight.

As the tail-chase went on, the FW got in close, and then, when Godfrey dropped his flaps to tighten his turn, he got aligned to fire; but the German, sensing Godfrey's superior position, kept swinging down in his turn, gaining speed and quickly pulling up, and with the advantage in height he then dove down on the American pilot. Time was in the German's favour. He could fight that way for an hour and still have enough fuel to land anywhere below him. Godfrey still had 400 miles of enemy territory to fly over before he could land. Knowing he had to be innovative, Godfrey raised his flaps, dove and then pulled up in a steep turn, while dropping his flaps slightly. The G force was severe, but the ploy worked, and he was confident of an imminent kill. Pressing the firing button he waited expectantly, but nothing happened, his guns weren't firing.

In taking this last gamble Godfrey had lost altitude but had been able to bring his guns to bear while flying below the FW. With the German's height advantage, he was able to come down, pull up sharply, and get on my tail again. The FW's 20mm cannons belched and Godfrey saw what looked like golf balls streaming by him. A little less deflection and those seemingly harmless golf balls would have exploded upon contact with the Mustang. 'Never turn your back on an enemy' was a byword with us, but Godfrey had no choice. Turning the plane over on its back, he yanked the stick to his gut. He left the throttle wide open as he dove. The needle stopped at 600 miles per—that was as far as it could go on the dial. Pulling out, he feared the wings would rip off, the plane was bucking so much. The last part of his pull-out brought the Mustang up into the clouds. Godfrey was thankful to have evaded the long-nosed FW, for that pilot was undoubtedly the best that he had ever encountered. He saw no other planes on the way homeback to Debden and had to wait until landing to hear the fate of my buddies.

"Bob Richards was flying on my wing over the Channel. He called me, 'Hello, Shirt Blue Red Leader, this is Red Two. My motor's acting up, am returning to base.'

'Roger, Red Two.'

"I didn't know it then, but those were the last words I was to hear from Bob.

"Motor difficulty was common [in] those days, and over the radio I could hear other boys reporting trouble. On approaching the Dutch coast my own engine started coughing and spitting. It was my turn now. Of the sixteen that took off that morning, only three from our squadron were able to meet the bombers over Berlin. Those three returned to the base. The three missing boys were from the other two squadrons. Weather was very bad over England. I started to let down through the clouds, but when ice formed on my wings, I turned back toward the Channel.

"Emerging from the clouds I flew south, letting down gradually until 500 feet above the Channel, then I turned back to England and flew at 600 feet just below the cloud base.

"Bob was not at Debden when I landed, but I didn't worry, and in fact gave no thought to it even an hour later when I still had no word. Probably he had landed at Martlesham Heath to see our friend J.J. and just forgot to call the base.

"I was still sitting in the dispersal hut when the phone in the intelligence room rang. I heard the low talking but the words were indistinct. Then Mac, the intelligence officer, approached me with a bottle and a glass. At the end of every mission a glass of whiskey was always given to the pilot, if he wished it, to settle his nerves.

" 'Here, Johnny, this is a bonus day. Have another drink.' I gladly accepted the offer of the free drink, but was suspicious of Mac, who didn't look into my eyes as he usually did when he handed a drink to me. His presence suddenly made me uncomfortable.

" 'Somebody's got to tell you, Johnny, and I guess I'm the one. A call just came through from the RAF. Bob's plane crashed at Framlingham. He was still in the cockpit. He's dead, Johnny.'

"His words hit me like a lightning bolt. It just didn't seem possible—not Bob, my war buddy. After living together for two years, our comradeship had strengthened into a love which for me was even greater than the feeling I had for my own brothers. We had shared everything, clothes, money, and yes, even girls. I knew his faults and merits just as he knew mine. I cried inwardly, but I didn't break down."

"There they are. You can learn to fly 'em on the way to the target", Blakeslee told his pilots that morning at Steeple Morden when they exchanged their P-47s for Mustangs. Ordinarily, American fighter pilots would have at least 200 hours of flying time in a Mustang before they were sent overseas to fly it in combat. The pilots of the 4th Fighter Group at Debden averaged just under forty minutes in the plane when they took it on their first operational mission over Europe. It was a lot to ask of them and, were it not for the fact that Colonel Blakeslee was going with them on virtually every mission, taking the same risks, at least some of them might have refused to go.

The risks they all took were certainly genuine. In addition to the constant hazards of air combat and German flak, they were largely unfamiliar with the P-51 and were having more than a reasonable share of engine failures due to overheating through coolant leaks. Such incidents resulted in the loss of several pilots and close calls for many more.

By the early spring of 1944, the fighter squadrons of the Eighth had nearly 1,000 Mustangs on strength and were dealing effectively with the various problems that had plagued the plane initially. The ever resourceful and occasionally brilliant crew chiefs and mechanics of Eighth Fighter Command often came up with elegant solutions in the field, fixes that brought the Mustang to a higher performance and safety standard. These on-the-spot improvements were communicated to North American engineering and assembly personnel in California who quickly incorporated them as changes to new aircraft on the factory line, which made for fighter deliveries that were closer to being combat-ready when they arrived in the war zone.

In little more than a year, the pilots of the 4th had progressed from operating Thunderbolts to a maximum combat radius of 175 miles and targets such as Paris and Brussels, to targets in the farthest reaches of Germany in their superb new Mustangs. They had hit their stride and were finally giving the pilots of Zemke's Wolfpack a real challenge.

The German Air Force could no longer count on being able to easily get at the American bombers when their Spitfire, Lightning, or Thunderbolt escorts were forced by range limitation to turn back for England. In the Mustang the American Eighth and Ninth Air Forces had a weapon with enormous fuel capacity and relatively low fuel consumption, enabling it to go all the way with the bombers and back, no matter where the target happened to be. When asked at the Nuremberg War Crimes Trials when it was he realized that Germany had lost the war, the Luftwaffe commander-in-chief Hermann Goering replied: "When I saw Mustang fighters over Berlin."

ON TO BERLIN

After the death of Bobby Richards, Lt. John Godfrey's long-time Army buddy, on one of the 4th Fighter Group's first Mustang missions, Godfrey grieved a while and then adjusted to the loss of his friend and got back to business. Godfrey's job as wingman to Capt. Don Gentile, who would become the group's highest scoring ace with a final total of twenty-three aerial victories, was to cover and protect his leader when Gentile went into aerial combat. In practice, however, it was more of a team effort, with the pair helping each other to accrue their high scores against the Luftwaffe.

In early March 1944, the 4th flew an escort mission to Berlin with their superb air leader and group commander, Col. Don Blakeslee, at the front of their formation.

United Press—London—March 8 American warplanes, 1,500 to 2,000 strong, made the greatest fire raid in history on Berlin today . . . Hundreds of Fortresses and Liberators, shielded by more hundreds of fighter planes, smashed through Hitler's most powerful defenses to lash Berlin . . . Desperate German Air Force fighters struggled in vain to defend the blow . . .

The American daylight precision bombing campaign against targets in German-occupied Europe began in the fall of 1942, complimenting the night bombing attacks of the British Royal Air Force. By the early spring of 1944, several USAAF heavy bomb groups were in place and operating their B-17s and B-24s from bases in the English Midlands and East Anglia. These American bases in the midst of the English countryside had names like Seething, Molesworth, Podington, Bassingbourn, Sudbury, Bungay, Deenethorpe, Kimbolton, Thorpe Abbotts, and Eye. They were named after villages they adjoined. The missions of their groups were set by the U.S. Eighth Air Force planners at Wycombe Abbey, a former girl's school in High Wycombe, Buckinghamshire, and the requirements for the raids came to the various bomb group stations via teleprinter the previous day. Preparation for the missions were implemented—with bombs, fuel and ammunition loaded, routes and timings set, crews briefed, etc, and then the operation was flown with the take-off usually in the pre-dawn hours. Assembly of these large aircraft formations was time-consuming but eventually the great bomber stream turned eastward for the flight into Europe.

The bombers bristled with machine guns and had been designed to defend themselves all the way to and from their targets, but that had not proved as effective as the planners had expected. The bombing campaign continued into 1944, when it was clear to the officers running the Eighth that the bomber crews could not adequately protect themselves against the German Air Force.

American losses in the bomber force were plainly unsustainable and something had to be changed in the system or the entire U.S. bombing effort would have to be suspended. It was at this point that the P-51 Mustang escort fighter began arriving at American fighter bases in England, in considerable numbers. It was hoped that the new Mustangs would be able to shepherd the bombers all the way to the deepest Continental targets and back in relative safety and with minimal losses to both bombers and fighters.

As the first box formation of the bombers approached the suburbs of the German capital, they were met by more than twenty ME-109 fighters. Gentile and Godfrey were part of the fighter unit at the front of the bomber stream that day and were immediately confronted by five of the enemy planes.

Johnny Godfrey was and always had been rebellious,

aggressive, and indifferent to authority, but he had come to like and respect Gentile, who was one of the few pilots in the group that he admired and would follow—one of the few, in fact, to whom he would listen. They had welded themselves into an effective team and one of history's greatest small fighting units.

Winston Churchill is said to have referred to them as: "The Damon and Pythias of the Air Force." Their history together included Godfrey's first combat mission, and the first time he had fired his guns in anger. It was because of his profound respect for Don Gentile's flying and fighting skills, and his impressive achievements in the air to that point, that John Godfrey acknowledged his wing leader as "the maestro" and was happy to fly as his number two. John Godfrey was a superb marksman and had the eyesight of an eagle.

Carefully, the pair began maneuvring with two of the 109s through a series of turns, sparring with them to get a sense of their capabilities. Godfrey was the first to get into firing position on the tail his Messerschmitt. : "Okay, I'll cover you," Gentile called to him on the radio telephone. Firing a few short bursts, Godfrey heard from his leader again: "Give 'em more . . .more!" He fired again and the 109 rolled onto its back. The German pilot bailed out.

Even for the experienced Gentile, the severity and violence of the turns they were engaged in was something new. These German pilots were clearly above average in their combat flying skills. Gentile managed to close to within 75 yards of a 109 and destroyed it with a few well-placed bursts. "Give me cover, Johnny, while I go after that 109 at two o'clock to us." "I'm with you" Godfrey answered. With the turns becoming more extreme, the pair were using their flaps now. Reaching 100 yards from the tail of the 109, Gentile fired and the German's cockpit instantly filled with smoke. The enemy pilot bailed out.

By now more than fifty German fighters were circling and making bold passes through the bomber stream. The gunners in the bombers were doing their best to defend their aircraft, but they clearly needed all the possible assistance from their "Little Friends" in the P-51s. Dozens of bright green flares streaked up from the B-17s and B-24s, signalling to the Mustang pilots that their big friends needed help desparately.

"All right, Johnny, there're two flying abreast at one o'clock. See 'em?" asked Gentile. "Yep," Godfrey replied. Gentile: Okay, you take the one on the right and I'll take the one on the left." Throttles to the firewall, both pilots advanced on their quarries. Taking no evasive action, the two 109s suddenly rolled away from each other, both aflame from the bullets of the two Mustangs. Between them, Godfrey and Gentile had now downed five Messerschmitts.

They climbed back to 22,000 feet to rejoin the bombers. Godfrey was the first to spot the next enemy aircraft. "Break, break starboard! One coming in at four o'clock to you." Together they broke to the right, passing the German head-on. "All right, Johnny. When he comes back around on the next turn, you break right and I'll break left." The apparently fearless 109 pilot came around again to take on the two Mustangs head-on. Gentile broke hard left; Godfrey right. They pulled into sharp, climbing turns to roar back down onto the German's tail. The 109 entered a steep dive aiming for the cloud layer below. They chased the German down for four miles through cloud and clear air, firing when they came close enough. All three of the planes pulled out at just under 500 feet, the Messerschmitt was trailing smoke. "You take him, Don. I'm out of ammo."

Hugging the treetops, the German pilot struggled to evade Gentile's Mustang, but he no longer had the speed to compete. Within range, the American fired again, striking the German's belly tank. The enemy pilot managed to climb a thousand feet before jettisoning his canopy and bailing out.

Godfrey then spotted a lone B-17 bomber out from their nine o'clock position, a straggler, evidently damaged and trying to make its way back to England with only occasional clouds for protection. Gentile and Godfrey were careful to refer to the B-17 only as "it", as they assumed that German ground stations would be listening in on AAF radio frequencies and, if they knew about the wounded bomber, would dispatch their own fighters to finish it off.

The buttocks of both Gentile and Godfrey ached and they longed to race back to the relative comfort of Debden. Knowing that the lives of the ten American aircrew in the limping B-17 depended on their help, however, the two fighter pilots drifted over toward the starboard wing of the hapless bomber. What protection they could offer was marginal as Godfrey's ammunition was entirely spent and Gentile's was nearly exhausted. They would have to slow way down and weave a lot to stay with the much slower bomber, which would add substantially to their return time, and all they could really do in the way of protection was to bluff any enemy fighters that might show up. Gentile waggled his wings to let the B-17 crew know that he and Godfrey would stick with them back to England.

Meanwhile, there was no shortage of action among the other pilots of the 4th. Lt. Allen Bunte of Eustis, Florida, a colourful character, lean and mean-looking, with the mustache of an old west outlaw, and an ambition to be an actor, was chasing five 109s down towards the ground and began firing at them when still 1,000 yards from the nearest one. He advanced to within 200 yards and his bullets found their mark. Just before Bunte lost sight of the enemy aircraft, it spun out and apparently crashed. Within minutes and while still flying at low altitude the American came upon a small German training plane breezing slowly over the wooded countryside. Determined not to allow the student to graduate, he fired on the light aircraft, and missed. Closing too rapidly on his intended victim, Bunte hopped over the German at the last second and turned back to witness the trainer settling into the canopy of trees they had been skimming.

A young pilot, a native of Altoona, Pennsylvania, Lt. Robert Tussey, was aloft on his second combat mission, flying near Magdeburg, Germany. The planes of his squadron had been widely scattered in the intensive air fighting and by chance Tussey happened to see a lone JU-88 heavy fighter/bomber flying ahead and moving in the same general direction. Inexperienced but careful, the P-51 pilot waited to be sure his identification of the plane was correct before closing in on it. He misjudged his approach slightly, overshooting somewhat. He throttled back until he was once again well positioned on the German's tail, and began shooting. Then he was being shot at as the tail gunner of the enemy craft let fly with a retaliatory stream of bullets that drifted over the American's wing.

An airfield came into view ahead of the two adversaries and the German pilot dived towards it, evidently thinking that gunners on the field would probably shoot the Mustang off his tail. The JU-88 twisted out of Tussey's gunsight image but was soon reacquired by him and this time when he fired, he watched as a single parachute appeared from the 88, which crashed seconds later taking the dead tail gunner in with it.

They brought the crippled bomber back as far as the English coast and Gentile contacted it: "Mustang to Fort. We'll be leaving you now. Good luck." The bomber pilot answered: "Thank you, very, very much, Little Friend." Arriving in the Debden area the two Mustangs broke and buzzed their squadron dispersal. According to Grover C. Hall, Jr., 4th Fighter Group public relations officer, "You could tell the veteran pilots from the newer ones by their conduct in the circuit. The tyros made long approaches to the landing strips, while the veteran hotrocks turned into the strip so short you'd swear the left wing was going to brush the ground."

Another March mission to Berlin for the 4th Fighter Group was led by Lt Col. James Clark. It was the third trip that Captain Nicholas 'Cowboy' Megura, of Ansonia, Connecticut, had made with the group to the Big B. Cowboy had a reputation as one of the 4th's most violent pilots in combat. He was there to fight Germans and made sure everyone in the group knew it. He was perceived as boisterous and somewhat disorderly, but he had downed two enemy planes on each of his two previous excursions to Berlin, as well as accounting for several planes destroyed on the ground and a few trains for good measure, and he was looking forward to adding to his score this day.

Clark now had the group climbing fast to come to the aid of a bomber formation that had just called for help. When the Mustangs arrived at the bombers, they were immediately bounced by five ME-109 fighters from out of the sun. In seconds Clark and Megura each destroyed a 109 and Cowboy was shot at by a third German, but shook him off. The American then noticed several enemy fighters attacking a straggling bomber roughly a mile away. He caught up with one of the attackers and was elated to see his rounds scoring on the engine of the target. Smoke began pouring from the German plane, whose pilot threw open his canopy, pulled back on the stick and stood up as if to bail out. But the German hesitated, probably wondering if he might still be able to land his burning fighter . . . if the American pilot might now break off the chase . . . or if his enemy might machine gun him in his parachute. Cowboy helped the German make up his mind by firing another short burst in his direction. The enemy pilot stepped out of cockpit and tumbled a few hundred feet before his parachute streamed open, jerking him upright.

The action had brought Cowboy quite low near an airfield outside of Berlin. Several ME-109s were circling in the landing pattern and Megura started following one of the German fighters, which didn't seem aware of his presence. Somehow none of the German pilots had noticed the enemy fighter over their airfield, so Cowboy lined up on one plane that had its flaps and landing gear down. Before he could shoot, however, two enemy fighters came racing across the field towards him, having suddenly recognized the Mustang profile. Megura fire-walled the P-51 but had trouble outrunning the German pair. He was finally able to outdistance them and headed back west at low level over Berlin, shooting up a train on his way.

As he crossed a low mountain range west of the city, he encountered six more enemy aircraft, evading them by weaving through some valleys. On course for Debden, he then came upon a Junkers JU-88 cruising at 10,000 feet. Cowboy chased it down to the roof-tops of the industrial area he was crossing. Only one of his guns was still working when he opened fire on the German. His last rounds were tracers and with them gone he pulled alongside the damaged plane. All he could do then was thumb his nose at the German pilot and yell something rude. Thirty days later, Megura was awarded the Distinguished Service Cross for his actions on that trip to Berlin.

HIGH ACHIEVERS

In the afternoon of November 20th 1944, Captain Jack Ilfrey led five P-51D Mustangs of the 20th Fighter Group to a rendezvous with two F5As (P-38 Lightning photo-reconnaissance aircraft), to protect them while they photographed Berlin and the surrounding area.

The weather was reasonably good, with 7/10 cloud cover, and the flak had been light thus far. When the F5s finished their primary assignment they headed south-west along the route of the Autobahn towards Magdeburg, taking more photos and attracting more intense flak.

They were to fly to Bonn, where American bombers had attacked airfields and synthetic oil facilities earlier in the day. However, the F5s were low on fuel and film and radioed that they were going to head for home. The overcast was becoming solid with only an occasional glimpse of the earth appearing.

It had become standard practice after escort missions for the Mustang pilots of the 20th to drop down on the deck and shoot up targets of opportunity on the way back to their base at King's Cliffe in the English Midlands. They had begun their operational tours of duty in the P-38 Lightning and had been completely sold on the plane. Many of them had resented having to convert to the P-51, but now, after several months with the Mustangs, they appreciated this finest of American fighters. "The P-51 made us feel like hunters in the skies over Germany. Our morale was high during ground strafing, chasing, or evading their fighters, during dogfights or just firing the guns. We also got an adrenline high."

The fighters spiralled down through a hole in the cloud cover and found an abundance of enemy trucks, tanks and other equipment heading for the front lines.

They flew west under the massive weather front, shooting

at various targets, expending a lot of ammunition and most of their fuel.

Captain Ilfrey told them to form on him and they would head for home. It was shortly after four p.m. Darkness comes early in northern Europe at that time of year. Uncertain of their exact position, Ilfrey set a course for England but figured that, with very little fuel remaining, they might have to land in Belgium or France. He decided they would stay low, below the weather front, as a stream of bombers might still be heading home through the overcast.

"We were in a good, tight formation. I was still trying to get my bearings when we came up on Maastricht, the Netherlands, which was still in German hands, and those hands began firing at us. We were headed north-west, so I veered right to get away from the city and all that ack-ack, but we were still picking up heavy fire, so we turned right again [east] to get away from all that ground action. At that point my wingman, Duane Kelso, radioed that he had been hit and was losing power. We were at around 700 or 800 feet in poor visibility when I happened to see a clear stretch which appeared to be a small emergency strip surrounded by trees. There were a few bombed-out buildings and a few wrecked aircraft scattered around. I pointed out the strip and told Kelso to try for it, and that I would cover him. Knowing we were almost out of ammunition and very low on fuel, I told the other pilots that they were on their own. They all made it OK to Belgium."

Ilfrey then instructed Kelso to use his own judgement about whether to try a wheels-down landing and, if he decided to do so and thought that Ilfrey could make it in there as well, to give him a "thumbs-up" signal as Ilfrey circled the field.

Kelso approached the short strip amidst heavy ground fire and made a rather hairy landing with wheels down, stopping near the edge of the trees. He ran from the Mustang as Ilfrey watched from overhead and continued to attract ground fire. Captain Ilfrey came around in a circle above the trees and Kelso gave his leader the thumbs-up signal.

Ilfrey: "I must have been out of my mind, but the thought of not going in never occurred to me. He was a good pilot, an excellent wingman. He would have followed me anywhere and I couldn't help feeling very close to him at that moment. Flashing through my mind was how Art Heiden and Jesse Carpenter had tried to pick me up when I had been shot down on a mission back in June, but they couldn't land because of the trees and the glider barriers where I had come down . . . what they must have thought when they had to leave me there deep in enemy-held territory. Friendships forged in combat are never forgotten."

Jack Ilfrey lowered his wheels and flaps and took his fighter, *Happy Jack's Go-Buggy*, in for an equally risky landing on the little strip. The Germans in the area were now firing on Kelso's plane and he quickly put a hundred yards between himself and the Mustang. He ran to the end of the strip, where Ilfrey would stop and turn around, ready for an immediate take-off, regardless of wind direction.

Ilfrey: "God, what a hairy landing, dodging holes, muddy as hell, but the *Go-Buggy* made it. I taxied a short distance up to Kelso, set the brakes, and jumped out on the wing. I took off my 'chute and dinghy and threw them away. Kelso got in and sat in what now was just a bucket seat lowered all the way down. We immediately discovered that four legs were not going to fit in the space and allow me full rudder control, so I stood up and he crossed his legs under him and I sat down on them.

There was not time to try other positions or adjust the seat and shoulder harness. I nearly scalped myself trying to close the canopy. Thank God it was a 'D'. So, there I was . . . head

and neck bent down, knees almost to my chin. As I closed
the canopy and turned the P-51 around to start the take-off
roll, we were well aware that ground troops were firing at us
and we were very tense. I yelled back at Kelso, 'Don't get an
erection or it'll push me out of here.' "

Ilfrey thought they were not going to clear the treetops. He
threw down more flaps and the Mustang pulled up just over
them. Fortunately, she had been light in fuel and ammunition. They made the short flight to Brussels and yet another
wild and difficult landing. That night they celebrated.

The next morning, hung over and still without a parachute
and dinghy, Captain Ilfrey brought the *Go-Buggy* back to
King's Cliffe. Kelso arrived a few days later by transport. At
King's Cliffe, Colonel Harold Rau, the group commander,
gave Ilfrey hell for "pulling a trick like that", jeopardizing
himself and his aircraft.

In all the ensuing years, Jack Ilfrey has not seen or heard
from Duane Kelso.

The motto of the famous American 4th Fighter Group of
World War Two was "4th but First." They could never have
made that claim were it not for Don Blakeslee taking charge
as their Commanding Officer in January 1944. Until then
they were second in every respect . . . in achievement, in
scoring against the German Air Force, in attitude and in
morale. Clearly, they needed someone to pull them into
shape, goad them into action, drive them into discipline, and
pound them into performance. Blakeslee was that man and
the Mustang was the plane for them. He saw to getting
Mustangs for his boys at the earliest possible date, and took
them into combat with their new planes that very day.

In his campaign to equip the 4th with Mustangs he was not
simply after a new toy for his boys, he had pure logic on his
side. When he compared the other Allied fighters of the day,

he pointed out that the Spitfire lacked range, the Hurricane lacked power and speed, the Lightning lacked manoeuvrability, and the Thunderbolt lacked speed in the climb and vital manoeuvrability against the German fighters. Only the Packard-Merlin Mustang was superior to its opponents in every respect, being faster than both the ME-109 and the FW-190 at practically any altitude and able to beat them both in a dive and a climb.

Before Blakeslee took command, the 56th Fighter Group, Hub Zemke's Wolfpack, was flying rings around the 4th, racking up records right and left and making the 4th look no better than second-rate. But all that was about to change. In the 4th, Blakeslee knew he had a rather rag-tag collection of talented, spirited, highly capable fighter pilots who simply needed what he could give them from his extensive experience. He brought them along rapidly, leading from the front, and was a magnificent role model in many respects. He and Zemke were, without question, the finest fighter leaders in the Air Force and with Blakeslee running the show, things soon turned around for the 4th. At the end of the European air war, the final scores were: 56th Fighter Group—976 enemy aircraft destroyed-air and ground, 4th Fighter Group—1,016 enemy aircraft destroyed-air and ground.

One of Blakeslee's greatest fighter pilots was Lt. Col. Jim Goodson, who remembered his commander: "Blakeslee was on every mission. Each pilot had only one thought in mind—not to let down Don Blakeslee. The new pilots put their faith in him; old hands like those of us who commanded the squadrons and often led the Group knew instinctively what he wanted; we were always where he wanted us and he was always where we knew he would be.

"When Blakeslee said 'Horseback here—I'm going in', he knew he would be covered. When any of us took our squadron into the attack, we knew we were covered. The disciplines of the RAF were ingrained in him."

American volunteers Don Gentile (pronounced Jen-tilly) and John Godfrey flew together as leader and wingman respectively, with the 4th Fighter Group and, at the end of their missions, the pair had accounted for at least fifty-eight enemy aircraft destroyed. Major Gentile had scored twenty-two air and six ground kills before he was returned to the United States to help raise money for the war effort. Major Godfrey was credited with eighteen air and twelve ground kills before he was shot down and made a prisoner of war.

Gentile recalled his combat flying in Mustangs with the 4th at Debden in 1944: "To show how a team works even when a big brawl has boiled the team down to two men flying wing on each other, Johnny and I spent twenty minutes over Berlin on March 8th and came out of there with six planes destroyed to our credit. I got a straggler and Johnny got one, and then I got another one fast. A Hun tried to out-turn me, and this was a mistake on his part. Not only can a Messerschmitt 109 not out-turn a Mustang in the upstairs air, but even if he had succeeded, there was Johnny back from his kill and sitting on my tail waiting to shoot him down. He was waiting, too, to knock down anybody who tried to bounce me off my kill.

"There were Huns all around. Berlin's air was cloudy with them. The gyrations this dying Hun was making forced me to violent action, but Johnny rode right along like a blocking back who could run with the best. After two Huns had blown up and another had bailed out, Johnny and I formed up tight and went against a team of two Messerschmitts. We came in line abreast and in a two-second burst finished off both of them. They were dead before they knew we were there.

"Then a Messerschmitt bounced Johnny. Johnny turned into him and I swung around to run interference for him. The Hun made a tight swing to get on Johnny's tail, saw me and rolled right under me before I could get a shot in. I rolled with him and fastened to his tail, but by that time we were very close to flak coming up from the city. The Hun wasn't so worried about the flak. I was his immediate and more desperate woe, but flak wasn't my idea of a cake to eat, and I didn't dare go slow in it while the Hun took a chance and put his flaps down to slow to a crawl.

"Then I got strikes on him. Glycol started coming out of him, and I had to pass him. But Johnny had fallen into formation right on my wing and he took up the shooting where I had left off. He put more bullets into the Hun while I was swinging up and around to run interference for him. Then he said his ammunition had run out and I said, 'OK, I'll finish him', and I followed the Nazi down into the streets, clobbering him until he pulled up and bailed out.

"The whole thing goes in a series of whooshes. There is no time to think. If you take time to think, you will not have time to act. There are a number of things your mind is doing while you are fighting—seeing, measuring, guessing, remembering, adding up this and that and worrying about one thing and another and taking this into account and that into account, rejecting this notion and accepting that notion. But it doesn't feel like thinking.

"After the fight is over you can look back on all the things you did and didn't do and see the reason behind each move. But while the fight is on, your mind feels empty and feels as if the flesh of it is sitting in your head, bunched up like muscle and quivering there.

"I remember . . . after I had run my score of destroyed to thirty, we were over Schweinfurt. and there were three Messerschmitts just sitting up there in front of me and not noticing me—just presenting themselves as the easiest shots I have had in this war so far. I was positive I was going to get all three.

"Then I saw a Hun clobbering a Mustang mate of mine. I dropped my easy kills and dove on the Hun to bounce him off that Mustang. I didn't think about it at all; it was just a reflex action—nor do I regret having such reflexes. If the feeling for team action had not been developed as a reflex in me—something I and all the other boys can do without thinking—then I would have been dead or a prisoner of war a long time ago."

Major Walter Konantz was flying Mustangs with the 55th Fighter Group based at Wormingford, England, on September 11th 1944. The group was escorting B-17s to Ruhland and were approaching the rendezvous point at 25,000 feet when he had to use the relief tube. In order to use the tube (which is vented overboard), it was necessary to unbuckle the lap belt and shoulder harness as well as the leg straps of the parachute, and slide well forward on the seat. He was in this position when a voice came over the radio shouting, 'ME-109s. Here they come.'

Konantz looked up and saw about fifty 109s diving through the American formation and firing. One crossed in front of him in a dive and was firing at a P-51 below and to his left. This was the first time he had ever seen an enemy aircraft and, with a case of 'buck fever', Konantz peeled off and went after him. The German saw Konantz chasing him and steepened his dive to the vertical. Konantz was also headed straight down with full power. Both aircraft descended from 25,000 feet at extremely high speed. Being completely unstrapped, Konantz was a free-floating object in the cockpit and his body was at zero gravity. The slightest movement of the stick would cause him to leave the seat and hit the canopy. The airplane was very touchy at this speed and at times he felt like a basketball being dribbled down the court.

"We both started to pull out at about 8,000 feet. I glanced

at my airspeed indicator which, at that moment, was showing 600 miles per hour, 95 miles per hour over the red line speed. The ME-109 had only completed about 45 degrees of his pull-up when his right wing came off through the wheel-well area. He spun into the ground in a few seconds with no time to bail out. Even though no one else saw this victory, and I didn't have any of it on the gun camera film,

I still got credit for it as one of the other pilots had counted the fires on the ground after the huge fifteen minute dogfight and reported to the debriefing officer that he counted thirty fires. There were claims of twenty-eight ME-109s shot down with the loss of two P-51s. After landing, when

I had stepped out onto the wing, my crew chief remarked, 'Better zip up your pants before you go in for debriefing.' "

Not all the heroes of the Mustang fighter groups were pilots. Master Sergeant Merle Olmsted was a crew chief with the 357th Fighter Group at Leiston, Suffolk, and recalled the routine there.

"Most Eighth Air Force fighter units assigned three men to each airplane. In addition to the crew chief, there was an assistant crew chief and an armament man. On arriving at the plane their first job was to remove the cockpit and wing covers and the pitot tube cover. Then the propeller was pulled through its arc and the pre-flight inspection began. The pre-flight is quite lengthy, consisting mostly of visual inspections, many of which were completed during the post-flight inspection the day before. All reservoirs were checked for fluid level, coolant, hydraulics, battery, engine oil and fuel. An inspection was always made under the aircraft for coolant leaks, which frequently occurred due to temperature changes. It was often difficult to tell coolant from water, but tasting a bit of the fluid will reveal the difference, as coolant has a bitter taste (and is poisonous if consumed in quantity).

"If all the visual and servicing checks were satisfactory, the engine was run, using the battery cart to save the airplane's internal battery. Because the seat is rather deep to accommodate the pilot's dinghy pack, a cushion in the seat helped the ground crewman to reach the brakes and to see out from the cockpit. Now the brakes were set and the seatbelt fastened around the control stick to provide 'up elevators' during the power check. The flaps were left down, the fuel selector was set to either main tank, the throttle cracked open, and the mixture control set to the idle cut-off position.

"After yelling 'clear' to be sure no one was near the nose of the plane, the starter switch was engaged (the P-51 has a direct-drive starter), along with engine prime. As soon as the cylinders began to fire, the mixture control was moved to 'run'. The propeller was already in 'full increase rpm' for the warm-up. Various additional checks were carried out, including checking that the engine oil and coolant temperature instruments were registering in 'the green'. The engine was run up to 2,300 rpm and the magnetos checked. With each mag off, the maximum allowable rpm drop was 100. The propeller governor was also checked at this rpm. The maximum rpm was 3,000, but this was for take-off and was not used on the ground run.

"After everything had checked out OK, the engine was shut down. The fuel and oil trucks cruised the perimeter track and all tanks were topped up. Now the windshield, canopy and rear-view mirror were all polished—and polished again. The armament man had long since charged his guns, so all aircraft on the field had 'hot' guns long before take-off. The gun switches in the cockpit were off, of course, but occasionally one was left on and the pilot gripping the stick could fire a burst, terrifying everyone within range, including himself.

"The pilots usually arrived fifteen to twenty minutes before engine start time, via an overloaded jeep or weapons carrier. After the pilot was strapped in with the help of the ground crew, his goggles and the windshield were given a final swipe. Engine start time came and sixty Merlins coughed into life around the airfield hardstands. Then the wheel chocks were pulled and, with a wave of his hand to the ground crew, each pilot guided his Mustang out to the proper place on the taxi track in a snake-like procession toward the active runway. The ground crews, and everyone else in the airfield area, sought a vantage point to watch the take-off, always an exciting event. The sight and sound of sixty or more overloaded Mustangs getting airborne was impressive.

"Much of the weight the planes were carrying was represented by two long-range fuel drop tanks, so vital to the success of the U.S. fighters in Europe. Most of these tanks were made of paper composition units, each holding 108 U.S. gallons and built in huge quantities by British companies. They were installed on the wing racks for the next day's mission the night before and were filled at that time. During operation they were pressurized to ensure positive feeding at altitude, by the exhaust side of the engine vacuum pump. The piping for this and the fuel flow is rubber tubes with glass elbows, which broke away cleanly when the tanks were dropped.

"Even though the drop tanks are pressurized, it was necessary to coax fuel into the system during the pre-flight. After switching to the 'drop tank' position, the engine would often die and the selector switch had to quickly be put back to 'main' and then to 'drop tank' until they fed properly. On the mission they were always dropped when empty, or earlier if combat demanded it. With all fifteen fighter groups operating, Eighth Air Force fighters could require 1,800 drop tanks per day.

"At mid-day, while the mission aircraft were out, the line

crews were in a state of suspended animation. It was mostly
free time, time to attend to laundry, read the squadron bulletin board to see when mail call was, and to see if your name
has appeared on any unwanted, but unavoidable, extra duty
rosters. There was also time to drop into the post exchange
for a candy bar, and to take in noon chow at the big consolidated mess hall.

"Regardless of what they had been doing while the mission was out, the aircraft ground crew would always 'sweat
out' the return of their particular aircraft and pilot, and when
both returned safely it was a great relief.

"Whether a crew had a close relationship with their pilot
depended on several factors—how long they had been
together, the pilot's general attitude towards enlisted men,
and if he was an outgoing individual. Although the word
'hero' probably never occurred to the ground crews, they
were well aware that it was their pilot who was doing the
fighting, and sometimes the dying. In most cases, there was
considerable affection for their pilot and they were proud of
his achievements. There was always a period of depression
when an aircraft and pilot failed to return from a mission,
and often the cause didn't filter down to the ground crew. In
a day or two, a new P-51 arrived, and a new pilot, and the war
went on.

"An average mission of the 357th Fighter Group lasted
about four to five hours and by the ETR (estimated time of
return) everyone was back on the hardstands. If the group
came into sight in proper formation and to the rising snarl of
many Merlins, it was probable that there had been no combat. If they straggled back in small groups, or individually, it
was certain that there had been some kind of action. Missing
red tape around the gun muzzles was a final confirmation.

"As each P-51 turned into its parking place, the pilot
blasted the tail around and shut down the engine, the wheels

were chocked and the mission was over—one more toward the completion of his tour.

"Now he brought any aircraft malfunctions to the attention of his ground crew, and left for debriefing. For the ground crews there was considerable work ahead to complete the post-flight inspection and repair the aircraft. If luck was with them, their airplane could be 'put to bed' in time for evening chow, and the work day would have come to an end. Often, though, it did not work out that way, and their jobs continued into the night."

Few people in Merle Olmsted's fighter group had been to the UK before being sent there in wartime. The personnel of the 357th FG found everything there different, the food, the cars, the people, and especially the weather. They had trouble understanding the English, and being understood by them; and they had difficulty with the money, but soon adjusted to both.

The first Mustangs received by the 357th were second-hand aircraft, B models passed on to them by the 354th FG, while Olmsted's group was still stationed at Raydon in Suffolk. Later, while based at Leiston, they would be equipped with P-51Ds which would proved extremely successful in their hands. But at first, the Mustangs were an unknown quantity to the pilots and ground crewmen of the 357th, all of whom had trained on the Bell P-39, an aeroplane they had come to know and not love. They soon came to appreciate, admire and respect the Mustang as they advanced through a variety of P-51 training schools including an RAF Merlin engine school.

Olmsted, a long-time friend of this author, said that in the Mustang they knew they had a winner. He recalled no major maintenance troubles with it. Relating it to the far more sophisticated fighters of the 1960s and 1970s, he referred to the P-51 as primitive and relatively trouble-free, compared to other fighters of the time such as the P-47 Thunderbolt. They did have some minor problems such as coolant leaks, but the only significant one they faced was engines running roughly due to the spark plugs of the time. He remembered that the British plugs were the best, but would give only about fifteen hours of fairly reliable operation, and that changing the intake plugs on a hot engine was always a difficult, demanding procedure.

Changing an engine on a P-51 was meant to take place after every 200 hours of operation, but Olmsted said that they rarely lasted that long under combat conditions. The engine life was reduced further after the group converted to 150 grade aviation fuel, which brought additional valve trouble and that in turn reduced engine life. But he was mightily impressed by the Merlin engine that powered the Mustang.

The workday of the ground crews on an American fighter field began early, usually before dawn. At Leiston, Merle and his fellow ground crewmen lived in huts a mile from the airfield. They made their way to the hardstands where their Mustangs were parked, by hitching rides on passing jeeps, weapons carriers or trucks. Some made the trip on RAF bicycles common found around the base, while others walked to work. For shelter on the normally brisk, blustery hardstands, it was common for ground crews to construct small shacks from the boxes in which belly tanks had been shipped. Some of the shacks were quite elaborate, containing bunks, workbenches, windows, and a few even had stoves that burned aircraft engine oil, but after a spate of line-shack fires caused by these contrivances, they were forbidden.

Olmsted: "The fourteen months on Eighth Fighter Command's Leiston airfield was a unique experience for the ground crews, and probably the high point of life for many. Most of us, however, did not appreciate this at the time, and wanted only to get it over with and go home. Only in later years did some realize what a fascinating time it had been, and many of us have returned several times to the now tranquil land that once housed a fighter group at war."

STROBELL AND OVERSTREET

Raydon Army Air Force Station 157 was located in Suffolk, near the east coast of England in 1944. The Ready Room bulletin board of the 351st Fighter Squadron, 353rd Fighter Group, showed Lt Robert Strobell and his fellow fighter pilots the names of those who would fly in combat each day. He recalled that if one's name did not appear on the combat board, you knew you would be assigned to other flying tasks like 'slow-timing' an airplane with a new engine just installed, similar to breaking in a new car engine. And some times one would be asked to take a plane to the depot for major repairs, or to train a replacement pilot on instruments, navigation, dive-bombing, or to fly a test-hop on a plane that had been running rough before repairs or adjustments had been made. Such assignments were given in the Ready Room.

The Ready Room was like a small theatre, with the seats facing a large map of most of England, the English Channel and western Europe. For security purposes, the map was covered when the pilots entered the room for a briefing. The map always had two colored lines on it, one showing the route of the bombers and another color for the route of the fighters and where they would rendezvous with the bombers. When the raid was to be a deep penetration into Germany, there was plenty of muttering and swearing among the pilots as the curtain went up. At one side of the map a bulletin board with large letters and numbers on it was readable from the back of the room. It displayed the take-off time, the combat altitude that to be flown, the compass heading to the rendezvous, and the compass heading for the return to base after the mission. The pilots were briefed on the weather over the mission area and the forecast for the base on their return, the bomber's mission, enemy movements if any, and sometimes a comment on what some of the other squadrons had done the day before. A lot of time and effort went into the planning and presentation of these briefings.

Of the routine, Strobell remembered that while sleeping in his Nissen hut, a pilot didn't have to worry about waking up in time for the next day's mission. He went to sleep in the knowledge that an orderly would come in at the appropriate time, wake him, tell him the time and when he was due in the Ready Room. The pilot got up, went to the latrine, dressed and walked (often in the mud) over to the Ready Room to find his assignment for the day posted on the big board. If he was assigned to a combat mission he would attend the briefing right after breakfast, and after the briefing, most of the pilots would visit the latrine again, some through nerves and others of necessity. He then picked up his parachute at the equipment room and went outside where a personnel truck with a canvas cover and bench seats on each side waited to take him and the other pilots out to the aircraft revetments. There the pilots were delivered to their airplanes spotted around the perimeter of the field. A crew chief waited there with each fighter. The crew chiefs had been alerted many hours before to the time of the flight and which planes would be flying that day. This was done on the telephone, conference-style, to all squadrons, so that the orders for the day only had to be read once.

Each pilot's crew chief briefed him on the status of his plane, usually 'ready' for combat, and warned you about the minor glitches such as a tail-wheel shimmy. He then helped the pilot climb up on the wing, don his parachute (some did this on the ground), and get settled in the cockpit. He assisted with the shoulder harness and seat belt.

If it was to be a combat mission, the pilot normally sat in the airplane for a few minutes, or as much as a half hour, waiting for the signal to start engines. Every pilot knew from the briefing what his position was in the flight, and on whose wing he would be flying, and he taxied out to the perimeter track in that position when his leader came by. The leader and wingman would then take off side by side, using the full width of the runway.

On returing from the mission, the pilot would taxi back to the same revetment and would tell his crew chief what he did on that mission, and most importantly, what the airplane did or did not do, and what needed to be repaired, or if it had any battle damage, bullet holes or flak hits that he was aware of—some pilots didn't know they had been hit. Then he hopped into a jeep or truck that took him back to the Ready Room.

If the pilot had fired his guns on the mission, the Intelligence Officer wanted to meet with him for a debriefing, particularly on enemy combat encounters, in which he had fired on an enemy aircraft in the air or on the ground. The whole process from beginning to end took from four to as much as eight hours, depending on the length of the mission and the complexity of the operation. The pilot then learned if he was scheduled to fly another mission, the second of the day. During his six months at Raydon, Bob Strobell flew two combat missions in one day on ten occasions.

A key role of the Allied fighter pilot in World War II was to shepherd his "big friends"—the bombers—to and from their targets in the various theaters of war. He did this with modest success for a while, but it was the advent of the ultra-long-range Mustang fighter that made the difference in the strategic bombing campaign.

One who flew the Mustang on the escort missions of the 357th Fighter Group was Captain William Overstreet, USAF (Ret): Bill reflected on how different the missions seemed after he had completed a few dozen. At first, everything was exciting—being awakened by the CQ, eating powdered eggs (usually green), going to the briefing room and seeing the tape across the map. So that's where we are going today. Worrying about how many German planes will come up to intercept the bombers and fighters? How good their flak gunners would be? Will we have a chance to go down and do some strafing? The pilots made notes to put on their knee pads, vital mission information. When and where do the fighters rendezvous with the bombers? What is the proper heading and how long will it take at X miles per hour? How strong is the wind and from what direction? Some fellas have been blown so far off course that they didn't have enough gas to get back to England.

They collect all of their equipment: mike, oxygen mask, the Mae West, raft, parachute and all of the other little things they may need. They climb on a weapons carrier for a ride out to the planes. It stops in front of Bill Overstreet's *Berlin Express* and he is greeted by Red Dodsworth and Whitey McKain, part of the crew who take care of his plane and make sure that everything is in the best shape possible. They have worked long and hard, and inform him that the *Express* runs smooth as a kitten. He hopes it will be a real tiger as just as well.

It is time to start engines. The weather—and ground visibility—is so poor that they want a crew chief to ride the wing and help guide Overstreet while he taxies out to the runway. Whitey is sitting on his wing, and after the engine is running Bill leaves the pad to follow Andy's [Captain Clarence E. Anderson] plane. He is flying Andy's wing today, and knows he will be with the best. Andy is already an ace and helps all of the pilots to gain confidence and be better in combat. Bill flew a lot with him while training in P-39s, and now, in best American fighter—the P-51—he feels that no one can out-fly them.

Overstreet has his canopy nearly closed to keep the snow

out as he taxies. He feels sorry for Whitey out on the wing in the snow. But, with Whitey's help, he makes it to the end of the runway and pulls up beside Andy's *Old Crow*. Andy is on the left side of the runway with Bill on the right a few feet away and a few feet behind him. Bill waves for Whitey to leave and concentrates on Andy's Mustang.

In the air, climbing in the clouds, Overstreet is staying as close to Andy as he can because if he loses sight of him even for an instant, Bill will be on his own in that cloud that have to climb through before I can see anything again. He remembers two friends who had a mid-air collision under these same circumstances and neither lived through it. That gives him plenty of incentive to stay close and concentrate.

This day Captain Overstreet feels they are lucky as the Mustangs break out of the clouds at 7,000 feet. The rest of the squadron is breaking out and forming up in flights of four. At full strength, each squadron would have four flights of four, and the group would have three squadrons. On this trip they don't have enough planes and pilots so there are only three flights and one spare in his squadron. Then Irv Smith calls on the radio. 'Sorry fellas, my engine is too rough. I have to abort.' So the spare man, Ernest Tiede, moves up to take Smith's place. Now Irv has to look for their base in the heavy clouds, with a rough engine.

The Mustangs continue climbing, heading for Muritz Lake where they are to meet up with the bombers at 12.40. With Overstreet as his wingman, Anderson has Joe Pierce and Bill Mitchell as his elements. The four have flown together for some time in P-39s and P-51s, and readily settle in for the hours of cold, uncomfortable sitting in the tight confines of their fighters, constantly alert to the possibility of an enemy surprise attack, a bounce from out of the sun when the German radar provides the information they need about the Mustangs' position and heading. That is why most missions are set in some general direction and later adjusted toward the specific target of the day. It's important to keep the enemy guessing if you can.

The American fighter pilots find the bombers just a few minutes behind schedule and in a somewhat loose formation. The three fighter squadrons take up their positions—one on the right—one on the left—and Overstreet's as the high squadron for this day. They are to stay above the bombers, making sure the German fighters don't have a high cover to attack the P-51s. With their height advantage, the Mustang pilots can dive to get more speed and break up any enemy formations that try to attack the bombers. The Americans gently weave at reduced speed to hold their positions with the bombers who are considerably slower.

Andy calls over the radio, 'Bogies at twelve o'clock—get ready to drop tanks.' He has sighted enemy fighters straight ahead of the Mustangs. The pilots then turn their fuel switches from our wing tanks, so they can drop their long-range external fuel tanks and prepare for combat. This, recalls Overstreet, was when everyone really got apprehensive. All of their training, everything they know, is about to be put to the test. The Germans still have a lot of good pilots and planes, and now roughly forty Americans are going to try to chase off about two hundred Jerries who are willing to do anything to keep the U.S. bombers from getting over their factories, refineries and other prime targets in their homeland.

At their leader's signal, the Mustang pilots drop their wing tanks, give the planes more throttle, and head for the German formation. They are lined up in waves of twenty abreast to go through the bombers using all their guns and cannon with plenty of targets for each of them.

Anderson picks out the enemy fighter that seems to be their leader and goes after him. Overstreet eases back on the throttle a little so he can watch behind Andy's plane and make sure that no one can get behind him. If a fighter can get behind another plane, his guns are much more accurate than at a wider deflection from other positions—why one always tries to get on the enemy's tail, and avoid letting him get behind you. A good fighter group is a team. Each man has his job and if everyone does his job well, the team effort is successful. Overstreet's job is to make sure that no enemy fighter gets in position behind Andy while Andy is trying to get behind the enemy.

At that point the other squadrons join the attack. Throttles are pushed forward for maximum power, climbing, diving, rolling, any possible maneuver to get a shot at the Germans while they are trying to do the same to the Americans. Andy gets hits on several of them and Bill getd a burst at a 109 that is too close to getting behind Andy. When Bill's .50 caliber rounds hits his tail, the German dives for the deck to get away from the Mustangs.

The scramble becomes really wild. All the Mustangs are chasing the German fighters and breaking away when the Germans get in position behind the Mustangs. That means making a fast, tight turn to deny Jerry a good shot. The sky seems full of planes in every conceivable position, frequently inverted, and Bill is firing whenever he thinks he is in position to get some hits.

The squadron succeeds in diverting most of the enemy, but a few get through to hit some of the bombers. A lot of planes are smoking—some of the American bombers and some of the German fighters—and parachutes are now blossoming as people leave their crippled planes.

After what seems an eternity to Overstreet, but is actually only about five minutes, the battle appears to be over, the remaining bombers are still heading for their target and the Mustangs are chasing any German fighters that haven't dived for the deck yet to get out of the fight. While most of the American fighters are scattered, Anderson and Overstreet are still together and the elements, Pierce and Mitchell, are still nearby. Andy sees some German fighters getting ready to hit the bombers again, so he and Overstreet head for them. Andy comes up below and behind a 109 and closes to within a few hundred yards. Bill keeps thinking he could fire but he waits until he is about 100 yards out before pulling the trigger. There is an explosion and the German's right wing falls off. He bales out while Bill fires at his victim's wingman. Sparkles light up on the fuselage and tail. The new target flips over and dives for the deck.

It is no longer such a target-rich environment, but Bill still counts ten German fighters trying to get to the bombers. The Germans see the Mustangs coming and decide to head for home. The Mustang pilots decide to give chase and follow the enemy planes in a power dive, pushing their air speed indicators to the red line. When one goes from 25,000 feet to the deck in a hurry, one is fighting trim tabs, rudders and everything else to keep flying straight, but all the pilots manage and Anderson is closing on one of the German planes when the enemy pilot pulls back on the stick and tries to lose his opponent by climbing. Andy stays right with him and Bill stays with Andy. The German tries every evasive tactic he can, but, when he and Andy are upside down, Andy gets a burst into the German's engine to end the encounter. With his engine on fire, the enemy pilot is forced to leave his aircraft.

Now they are a few thousand feet over Germany, the German planes are scattered in all directions, and the group was spread all over the map. A decision has to be made—do the Mustangs go back up to see if they can help any bombers who may have lost engines and can't keep up with their formation? They are sitting ducks for enemy fighters, so some P-51s escorting them could make the difference to their survival. Or should they stay on the deck and look for trains, barges, ammunition dumps or military convoys to attack?

As the P-51s are low on ammunition, the pilots start climbing. Soon, Pierce and Mitchell join Andy and Bill, and after all of the action, the flight is together to start the return trip to England, and will offer assistance to any 'wounded' bombers they see. They try to avoid the areas of heavy flak.

They spot and stay with a bomber that has lost two engines, until they near the English Channel and feel the bomber crew can make it from there. The Mustangs have just enough fuel to get back to base. There are still a lot of clouds over England, but now the ceiling is almost 100 feet so they have no trouble getting to base and landing.

There is no way anyone could count the planes they shot at, or those that shot at them, or the number of radar-guided ground gunners firing at them, or how many times they had an enemy plane in their sights, but had to break off because an enemy plane was closing behind from behind. How many times did they have to break off to chase one who was closing in on one of their teammates? A dogfight is almost a blur because of the fast and furious action. Today's mission lasted a little over five hours. The P-51s destroyed sixteen German planes, and one American pilot had to bail out over Germany. Overstreet is grateful and relieved to be back safely.

THREE TURNING, ONE BURNING

The Boeing B-29 would ultimately become an excellent bomber, the best heavy bomber of the war, in the opinions of many airmen and aviation writers. But throughout its development and the early part of its operational history, its crews had to contend with one terrible flaw—its Wright R-3350 engines. For much of the aeroplane's operational span, wags referred to it as "three turning, one burning", a moniker it had earned in flight testing.

The R-3350 was designed in 1937 and its initial testing greatly impressed the Army Air Corps, but it was still not in mass production by 1940 when many in Washington expected the United States to be at war in the near future. A sudden urgency on the part of the Army to complete the development and full-scale production of the powerplant, led to haste in the effort and some serious and persistent problems. Rushing the programme in the pressures of the pre-war period cost the lives of many airmen and threatened the success of the whole B-29 project. Boeing was caught up in a seemingly endless series of design changes on the bomber and had to concurrently cope with the continuing engine troubles.

Of primary concern to Boeing chief test pilot Edmund 'Eddie' Allen when he started the flight testing of the XB-29 in September 1942, were the engineering projections that the engines were likely to dangerously overheat after merely an hour or so of operation. But his impression of the aeroplane's performance through the first eighteen hours of flight testing remained essentially favourable. On December 28th, however, Allen was forced to prematurely abort a test flight of the prototype when the number one engine caught fire.

Another engine fire occurred two days later during the initial test flight of the number two XB-29, which caused suspension of the flight testing until February 18th. Allen resumed flight testing that day and, tragically, experienced two in-flight engine fires on the second test aeroplane. Then, declaring an emergency, he tried to return to Boeing Field, but the raging fire burned through the wing. Allen, his entire eleven-man engineering flight crew, nineteen workers at the Frye Packing Plant near the airfield, and five firemen, died when the big plane fell on the packing plant after breaking up in the air.

At the Wright aero engine company, an intensive effort was under way to correct the problems with the R-3350. The engine fires persisted through 1943, causing the loss of nineteen early-production B-29s, before two new marks of the power-plant were introduced with modifications that did reduce the tendency of the engines to overheat, and the related fire incidents. The extent of such incidents was reduced but not eliminated.

Engine fires continued to occur together with mounting aircraft and crew losses. Wright engineers then designed new baffles to enhance engine cooling and this dramatically improved the reliability and safety of the aeroplane, an improvement critical to its eventual success in the strategic bombing campaign against Japan.

Theirs was one of the most demanding jobs of Mustang pilots in the Second World War. They flew the missions of the Very Long Range (VLR) fighter groups, the 15th, 21st and the 506th Fighter Groups of the U.S. Army Air Force's VII Fighter Command, the 'Sun Setters'. These trips primarily involved the escorting and protection of the B-29 heavy bombers in their attacks on Tokyo and more than fifty other Japanese target cities between April and August 1945. In addition to the escort role, they would later be assigned to hit ground targets including airfields, ship, road and rail traffic, and enemy facilities, in preparation for the long anticipated Allied invasion of the Japanese home islands.

Based on the hard-won island of Iwo Jima 650 miles south of Tokyo, the Japanese capital, the Sun Setters accompanied the American heavies fifty-one times on their exhausting visits to Japan and the Bonin Islands. Iwo Jima is a tiny island that is strategically located to provide both a base for the fighters that would protect the B-29s on their lengthy raids, and a sanctuary for the bombers that were damaged or short of fuel on their return flights to the Marianas. In the campaign, they engaged and destroyed 234 enemy aircraft in aerial combat and accounted for the destruction of a further 219 e/a on the ground. They suffered the loss of 99 pilots killed and 131 Mustangs shot down.

The P-51 Mustang was considered one of the most agile and manoeuvrable fighter planes of the war, but it did not handle nearly so well when full of fuel. It was equipped with internal fuel tanks in both wings, a fuselage tank behind the pilot's seat, and a 110-gallon drop tank under each wing. While the fuselage fuel tank was still full, the aeroplane was tail-heavy and somewhat sluggish, and it was vital to burn off most of the fuel in this tank before taking on enemy aircraft in combat. It was also important to use the fuel of the drop tanks before entering air combat, as they would have to be jettisoned for best performance in action. The Mustang pilot then had to rely entirely on his remaining internal fuel supply for combat and his return flight to Iwo.

With its astonishingly great range, speed, reliability, fire power, and relative ease of maintenance, the Mustang proved the ideal fighter for this unique effort. These P-51s were, for the most part, flown by experienced combat pilots or men with many hundreds of hours as Mustang training instructors. They formed what they called 'the Tokyo Club', composed of P-51 pilots who had made the 1,300+ mile round-trip, frequently through rough weather, in their single-engined fighters to the enemy target cities that were fanatically defended by Japanese Imperial Air Force and Navy fighters. The Mustang pilots had to defend the bombers from the enemy aircraft, fighting their way to and from the targets, while occasionally suffering battle damage and always sweating out limited fuel, navigating across vast expanses of open sea, and the unimaginable fatigue of an eight-hour flight in a throbbing, roaring cockpit environment.

The contributions of the P-51 fighter and B-29 bomber to the successful conclusion of the Second World War for the Allies were immensely important. In the Pacific theatre of war, the Japanese continued to pursue victory at the end of 1944 despite the utter hopelessness of their military situation. Their military leaders determined to exact an enormous price in Allied lives and equipment by requiring their western enemies to mount and carry out a massive invasion of the Japanese islands rather than submit to the shame of surrendering on the Allies' terms.

The American president Franklin D. Roosevelt had died in office on April 12th 1945, and Vice President Harry S. Truman, a then unknown quantity, took over the crucial U.S. war effort at a sensitive moment. One of his earliest briefings as president informed him of the existence of the American atomic bomb and its anticipated capability for the destruction of an entire major city. He was immediately thrust into decision-making about the possible use of the new weapon in the war. One consideration involved the pros and cons of invading the Japanese islands and the projected million or more Allied casualties. Should the Allies move ahead toward such an invasion? Should they instead try to bring about an end to the hostilities through the employment of the new and as yet untested atom bomb against one or more Japanese cities to force an unconditional surrender? Truman would soon have to decide.

In a commitment to President Roosevelt, his commander-in-chief, AAF General Henry H. Arnold had established the Twentieth Air Force to achieve "the earliest possible progressive destruction and dislocation of the Japanese military, industrial and economic systems and to undermine the morale of the Japanese people to a point where their capacity for war is decisively defeated." In return, Arnold was given total control of the B-29s in the China-Burma-India Theatre of Operations.

In late August 1944, Major-General Curtis E. LeMay arrived in the CBI to take charge of XX Bomber Command, and later XXI Bomber Command, and the American bombing campaign against Japan. He had served in England where, as commander of the Third Bomb Division of the Eighth Air Force and had played a major role in the success of the daylight strategic bombing of Germany. From the new B-29 bases of Guam, Saipan, and Tinian in the Marianas island group, LeMay brought in a number procedural changes including target marking by Pathfinder aircraft, and other reforms. But B-29 crew and aircraft losses were rising in the high-altitude daylight attacks without producing the desired results.

Ultimately, LeMay concentrated all the B-29 operations against Japan in a series of ferocious fire raids that were even more extreme than the earlier fire-storm attacks on German target cities. The highly combustible wood and paper structures of Tokyo and the other Japanese cities and towns would prove optimal targets for his B-29s, which had sufficient "legs" and bomb-load capacity to bring enormous quantities of incendiary bombs over great ocean distances to hit Japan hard and often, and make her burn.

The first trial of LeMay's fire raids on Japan occurred on the night of 9/10 March 1945, when 279 B-29 Superfortress bombers were dispatched to attack Tokyo. When the raid began, surface winds were gusting at 30 mph and the fires started by the thousands of incendiaries dropped from the bombers spread rapidly, creating the same sort of firestorm that had engulfed Hamburg in the British and American raids of July 1943. In this most destructive conventional air raid in history, sixteen square miles of Tokyo were destroyed and 84,000 people killed.

American Marines began an invasion of Japanese-held Iwo Jima on February 19th 1945, a bloody battle that would take thirty-six days and 6,821 American lives. The Americans had to deal with 23,000 Japanese defenders occupying the island. The airfields on Iwo were badly damaged and useless following the fighting. After the battle, U.S. construction battalions immediately began work there on an airfield for the P-51 Mustangs of the 15th and 21st Fighter Groups which would be assigned to the escort of the B-29s of XX Bomber Command. Iwo's location enabled the round-trip to Tokyo for the Mustangs, but the volcanic dust of the airfield created problems with visibility in taxying and take-offs along with clogged filters in the planes.

In the night of March 27th, the pilots and enlisted men of VII Fighter Command on Iwo were awakened before dawn to small arms fire and screaming from Japanese hold-outs who had come down from their caves to infiltrate the American camp. With maniacal fervour, they used samurai swords to slash at the enemy tents, spreading confusion as the pilots scrambled for weapons to repel the attack. The combined Marine and Army Air Force personnel gradually eliminated the enemy resistance, killing 333 Japanese troops while losing forty-four Americans and suffering eighty- eight wounded.

The first mission in which the Mustangs shepherded the

B-29s took place on April 7th, when 108 P-51Ds left Iwo to rendezvous with more than 100 of the big bombers at Kozu, heading for the Nakajima aircraft engine factory at Tokyo. Seventeen of the fighters were forced to abort the 1,320-mile mission. Navigation for the Mustang pilots was provided by three accompanying B-29s on both the entire outbound and inbound legs of the trip. These navigational bombers carried additional life rafts to be dropped to any Mustang pilot who might have to come down in the sea. The U.S. Navy also participated by positioning some of its submarines along the route of the Mustangs, ready to pick up any such unfortunate airmen.

Flying in a formation of staggered vees, the B-29s, which had come to be referred to as "B-san" or "Mr. B" by the Japanese citizenry, were protected by many flights of four Mustangs each which climbed to positions above and to the flanks of the bombers. From these positions the fighters began weaving to maintain pace with the bombers and to keep watch on each other's tails in case any Japanese fighters should try to bounce them from above.

The B-29s were cruising at 15,000 feet, covered by the Mustangs which were staggered between 17,800 and 20,000 feet within ten minutes after rendezvousing with the bombers. As the formations crossed Sagami Bay between Atami and Hiratsuka, they were greeted by a profusion of Japanese fighters rushing to the attack. Tony's, Tojos, Nicks, Irvings and Zekes arrived and tried to bore through the bomber stream.

At that moment, twenty P-51s of the 15th Fighter Group dropped their long-range fuel tanks and closed on the enemy aircraft, Major Gil Snipes in the lead. Dropping his tanks, Snipes experienced engine failure. His Mustang fell for nearly two minutes before he was able to restart the Merlin. He had lost several thousand feet of altitude and precious time while climbing back to the melee above. Rejoining his wing-man, Snipes spotted and lined up on a pair of Tojos that were flying line abreast. Firing on one of the enemy planes, he saw it begin to trail smoke, but was rapidly overruning his victim and soon lost sight of him. But it was immediately replaced by another Tojo inviting his attentions. A quick burst caused the enemy plane to disintegrate, with the pilot managing to bail out.

As the giant American formation approached Tokyo, one of the B-29s was attacked by a twin-engined Japanese aircraft which dropped a phosphorous bomb on it. A Mustang attacked the enemy plane head-on, setting it alight and sending it downward.

As things so often happen in wartime, a foul-up occurred when Lt. Charles Heil lost contact with the three navigational B-29s and became separated from the other Mustangs of his squadron. He soon located and tacked on to another section of P-51s, not realizing that these fighters were, in fact, accompanying a different formation of bombers on their way to hit a target at Nagoya. When he believed they had reached the rendezvous point, he saw plenty of B-29s all around him, but no additional P-51s. Heil continued to fly with the bombers in the belief that they were headed for Tokyo.

As the whole force turned onto the bomb run, Heil's engine began to misfire and he immediately contacted one of the nearby B-29s to inform the bomber pilot that he could not continue with them. The bomber crew then jettisoned its bomb load and turned back towards Iwo to shepherd the malfunctioning Mustang. The fighter and bomber made it safely back to Heil's base, where he discovered that he had actually been to Nagoya instead of Tokyo.

In the Tokyo raid itself, the Mustang escorts shot down twenty-one Japanese fighters for the loss of one P-51. One other Mustang failed to return to Iwo Jima. Low on fuel 200 miles north of Iwo, the pilot, Lt. Frank Ayres, bailed out and was immediately picked up by a U.S. Navy destroyer. It would not be Lt. Ayres' only contact with the American air-sea rescue operation.

Ayres was leading a flight of Mustangs on high cover over a fighter strike on June 23rd. The target was the airfield at Shimodate. Enemy aircraft rose to meet his flight and in the action, Lt. Ayres shot down one of them and turned to chase a second fighter down to 6,000 feet where he lost it in the clouds. He then encountered another enemy aircraft and his Mustang was damaged in the ensuing fight. He headed away from the target airfield, his engine shot up and his radio hit and unusable. He turned on a heading toward a point where he knew a U.S. submarine was on station to rescue downed Allied pilots. He located the position of the submarine and bailed out, landing in the sea within 100 yards of the sub. He was hauled on board before even having time to inflate his dinghy.

One of the Mustang pilots that day, Major James Tapp, was credited with the destruction of four enemy aircraft on the mission, and with damaging another. After his combats, he noticed a nearby B-29 that was obviously damaged and heading for the coast. It was being harassed by a Ki-43 Oscar, a slow and relatively fragile Japanese Army fighter, when Tapp intervened and soon shot the Oscar to pieces in a head-on pass. Tapp and his wingman then took on the job of protecting the crippled B-29, which was soon under attack again, this time by six assorted Japanese fighters. The Mustang pilots quickly broke up the party and shot a wing off one of the attackers. The bomber continued on to its base arriving there safely, if long overdue. At the giant B-29 base on Tinian island, there was elation among the American bomber crews over the success of their effort and, in partic-ular, the difference made in their safety and survival by the presence of their greatly appreciated Mustang escort.

By May, the Mustangs of the 506th Fighter Group had joined those of the other two groups on the escort missions to Japan. The hazards of these operations was underscored for the American fighter pilots during the mission of June 1st. 148 Mustangs were climbing to join a large force of XXI Bomber Command B-29s on the way to a maximum effort attack on a target at Osaka.

Two hours into the flight the fighters entered an enormous weather front which towered beyond 23,000 feet. In the minimal visibility and violent turbulence, several mid-air collisions occurred, and many of the pilots became totally disoriented, their instruments toppling, their wings and control surfaces icing up. Strung out, with many of them lost, just twenty-seven of the original fighter force managed to locate and join up with the B-29 formation as it continued on course to Japan. More than ninety of the Mustangs were forced to abort and head back towards Iwo. Twenty-four of these simply disappeared and were not heard from again. Two of the fighter pilots bailed out when their aircraft ran out of fuel, but both were picked up by air-sea rescue ships.

In the weeks that followed, the Mustangs of VII Fighter Command performed brilliantly in the role of protecting the big B-29s to and from their Japanese targets, but, in the view of General LeMay, these high-altitude strikes were simply not producing results on the scale that was required. LeMay then elected to switch from daylight precision bombing with high-explosives from high altitude, to low-level night drops of incendiaries. The change was dramatic and profoundly successful, and also resulted in the re-assignment of the Mustangs to attacking Japanese airfields. They continued to engage many enemy fighters in the air near the fields, but also strafed, and rocketed many aircraft on the ground.

The final Mustang escort mission of the war was flown on

August 10th 1945, the day after the second atomic bomb was exploded over Nagasaki, and four days after the first such weapon had been exploded over Hiroshima. On the U.S. escort mission to Tokyo of the 10th, P-51s of the 15th and 506th Fighter Groups downed six enemy aircraft. The protection provided by the Mustangs to the crews of the B-29s saved hundreds, possibly thousands of American airmen. Still, in spite of all the precision bombing strikes, the mining operations, and the massive fire raids, the unconditional surrender the Americans had been anticipating from the Japanese failed to materialise. In the end it took the devastation of two Japanese cities by B-29-delivered atomic bombs, and the threat of additional atom bombing, to bring Japanese officials to the peace table aboard the battleship USS *Missouri* in Tokyo harbour.

DOUBLE-BIRD

The American engine of war production was running at full throttle in 1943. The pace of warplane making reached a peak and the Mustang-maker North American Aviation was employing more than 84,600 factory workers in its Inglewood, California, Dallas, Texas, and Kansas City, Missouri plants. The company was on its way to building more warplanes—fighters, trainers and bombers—than any other American airplane maker in the Second World War.

In that same year the flight test air crew and engineers were bringing the giant new Boeing B-29 Superfortress bomber through its performance evaluations and early teething problems. The plane, in great numbers, was destined for the very long ranging attacks of the American bombing campaign against Japan in the final months of the war. There would be many problems associated with the precedent-setting mission of the new bombers, not least being the matter of providing effective fighter escort protection for them over the vast expanse of ocean from the massive Tinian air base in the Marianas to the Japanese home islands and back.

Only the North American P-51 Mustang, of all the fighters in the USAAF inventory, was capable of making the long, and arduous trip, but doing so on a routine daily basis was believed to be too much to expect of the fighter pilots who would have to sit for eight hours or more and be ready to defend their charges in combat. The fatigue factor would simply go beyond excessive. To deal with the problem, the design engineers of North American got busy on a unique solution, a new, ultra-long-range fighter that would carry a second pilot to share the flying duties.

The new plane would be designated the P-82 and referred to as the "Twin Mustang." Basically, the design incorporated the fuselages of two P-51H Mustangs which were connected by a constant-chord wing. Their tails were joined by a single rectangular tailplane and standard port and starboard outer wing sections were employed. The plane was flown by a pilot in the port fuselage sections; the copilot sat in the starboard cockpit. Both of the cockpits were, however, fully equipped, enabling the pilots to fly the plane from either cockpit and spell each other on very long flights.

The so-called Twin Mustang was actually a new design. Mustang designer Edgar Schmued added a 57" fuselage plug immediately behind the cockpit areas of each fuselage, to accommodate the installation of additional fuel tanks and other equipment. The new centre wing section was an entirely new design and would house the M2 Browning machine-gun armament. The outer wing sections were substantially strengthened to carry new hard points for additional fuel drop tanks or up to 1,000 lb of ordnance. New, enlarged dorsal fillets were added to the two vertical tail fins to increase stability in the event of an engine failure.

The P-82 was designed to be powered by two Packard-built V-1650 Merlin engines which would ultimately be replaced with Allison V-1710 engines of 1,600 horsepower each, with counter-rotating propellers. The first two prototype aircraft and the next twenty P-82B models were, in fact, powered by the Packard Merlins. In early testing engineers found the arrangement inadequate, requiring a major month-long rethink. This, coupled with an increase in the licensing cost paid to Rolls-Royce for each Packard-built Merlin made in the United States, led the U.S. Army to negotiate an agreement with the Allison Division of General Motors for a new version of the V-1710-100 engine, a slightly lower- powered engine than the Merlin it was replacing. North American was then required to switch to the all new Allison for installation in all P-82C and later models of the plane. Subsequent per-

Mustang pilots of the 357th Fighter Group return to their base at Leiston
in Suffolk, England, after escorting bombers of the Eighth Air Force on
a deep penetration raid into Germany in 1944.

A cannon-armed factory-fresh P-51A at Inglewood, California, awaiting delivery to the U.S. Army Air Force. The same North American Aviation plant had produced the B-25 Mitchell bombers in the background.

A North American Aviation factory assembly line with early Mustangs under construction.

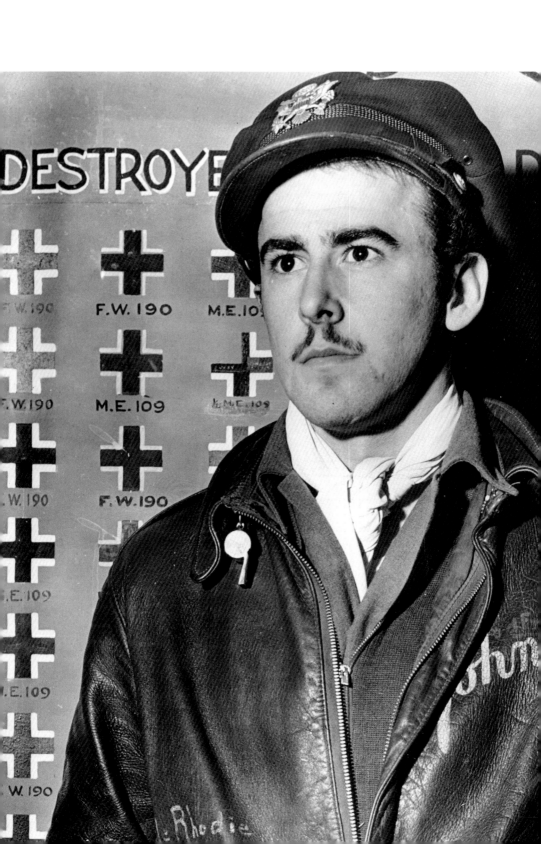

At left, Captain John Godfrey, who flew as wingman to Captain Don Gentile in the 4th Fighter Group at Debden, Essex, England during the Second World War. Godfrey was credited with downing eighteen enemy aircraft. Above: Armourers reloading the .50 calibre guns of a P-51 Mustang.

Duke, the 334th Fighter Squadron dog at Debden, in the seat normally occupied by Ralph "Kidd" Hofer, who is being interviewed by American newspaper reporter on the wing of Hofer's *Salem Representative;* right: Eighth Fighter Command mission board with wing assignments.

The other principal American fighters in the European Theater of the Second World War were, top left, the Republic P-47 Thunderbolt and, bottom left, the Lockheed P-38 Lightning. Above: Colonel Don Blakeslee, commanding officer of the 4th Fighter Group, Eighth Air Force.

Major Pierce McKennon, 4th Fighter Group, with his P-51, *Ridge Runner*.
Right, the clean, efficient design of the Focke Wulf Fw190 cockpit.

P-51Ds of the 4th Fighter Group in formation over England in 1944. Right, Captain Jack Ilfrey of the 20th Fighter Group based at King's Cliffe, England. In one of the most daring acts of the war, Captain Ilfrey landed his Mustang in a small field to rescue his downed wingman, Duane Kelso.

At right, Bob Hoover who, for many years, demonstrated the company-owned Mustang for North American Aviation. Bottom right: *Batty Betty*, a postwar P-51 racer.

In the dispersal hut of the 336th Fighter Squadron, 4th Fighter Group at
Debden, England. It is the oddly quiet, nervous time before a mission.

formance testing then established that the Allison-powered P-82s had a lower top speed and less efficient high altitude performance than their Merlin-powered predecessors. The earlier Merlin P-82s were relegated to trainer roles.

Each main landing gear leg was attached to the front wing spar beneath the outboard side of each fuselage, the wheels retracting inward under the fuselage and wing. Initially, the plane would be armed with six .50-calibre machine-guns mounted in the centre wing section.

Early design work on the new plane began in October 1943 with a fundamental range requirement of 2,000 miles without refuelling. Work was started on the two prototype XP-82s in January 1944 and the first flight came on June 26th 1945 and the aircraft was accepted by the Army Air Force on August 30th. AAF officials had been so impressed with the aircraft in its early development that they placed the initial order three months before the first flight of the prototype.

At North American Aviation, the approach to getting a new aircraft type into the air was a cautious, careful, reasoned affair. In the case of the XP-82 prototype, the initial step toward the flight test was an official engineering acceptance inspection made on May 25th 1945 at the Inglewood plant, at Mines Field, which is now the Los Angeles International Airport site.

NAA test pilot Joe Barton was scheduled to take the prototype up on her first flight from the 4,500 main runway at Mines, and no one involved that day was expecting any trouble. But when Barton had completed a series of taxi tests and ground runs at gradually increasing speeds, he turned the factory-fresh Twin Mustang onto the runway to begin its first ever actual take-off roll. As the plane neared lift-off speed he pulled back on the control stick as far as he dared, and then as far as he could, and the airplane remained firmly on the ground. Over several days he tried repeatedly to make the plane take-off, without success. The technical brains of the company met to consider the problem. Chief Engineer Ray Rice, chief of the engineering technical section Larry Waite, aerodynamicist Ed Horkey, chief test pilot Ed Virgin, Mustang designer Edgar Schmued, and Mustang test pilot / Merlin engine specialist Bob Chilton were all in attendance. Chilton tried to make the bird fly. It wouldn't. Once again, Joe Barton tried a new series of take-off tests, to no avail.

When the weekend came, Barton and Ed Virgin decided to try and fly the plane in the relatively quieter, less busy hours of Saturday and they had most of the fuel off-loaded to see if improved acceleration from the reduced weight might help. The pressure was on to get the seemingly recalcitrant machine airborne. Roaring down the runway, Barton brought the stick back more and more until it was nearly fully back when, without warning, the big plane suddenly leapt off the ground and was instantly at an altitude of fifty feet. The surprised Barton quickly recovered and safely continued the short flight.

Chilton: "The engines were set up with the propellers rotating towards each other. Dut to the direction of travel, a stall was set up with the airplane center section. Then they swapped engines left to right and right to left. I flew it ten days later and it became like a normal P-51."

Horkey: "What was happening was that we had propellers rotating in different directions on the left and right engines. For some reason, which I can't remember, we started with the blades moving upward in front of the center section. What this does, particularly at high angles of attack, is to create upward flow approaching the leading edge of the center section of the wing. You also have normal upflow ahead of the wing. The two upflows would add together and we got an early stall. The center section area represented a large portion of the wing area. So what was happening was that we were stalling out early and just not getting enough lift. It wasn't any mysterious vacuum holding it down or anything like that. It was just a standard stall or the wing section. I remember taking a ride during this period in one of the fuselages, and we had tufts on the wing. You could see the stalled flow. It would also happen at high-speed turns. We changed the [propeller] rotations to go down in the middle and we had the problem solved."

Work progressed through the year, but delays in delivery of engines to the waiting airframes at Inglewood plant meant that none of the P-82s would see service in the war.

The order book of North American showed 500 of the new planes to be built as P-82Bs, but with the end of the war on September 2nd, the order was cancelled except for twenty of the aircraft. During their construction in 1946, it was decided to fit two of them with large radar nacelles under the centre wing section to test them in the night-fighter role. The night-fighters were built with a modified starboard cockpit for a radar- intercept observer instead of a copilot.

With the expansion of a procurement budget, the order was then increased to 250, with 100 being built as long-range escort fighters and 150 as night-fighters. The P-82s would soon replace aging Northrop P-61 Black Widows, which suffered a persistent shortage of spare parts along with a seemingly everpresent need for maintenance, making them very difficult and expensive to keep airworthy.

At the height of the Allied round-the-clock bombing offensive against Germany in 1944, the P-51 Mustang showed both sides in the conflict that a well-designed, long-range single engine escort fighter with one pilot could do the job formerly believed to be exclusive to a twin-engined aircraft with a crew of two. But with the advent of the B-29, and the even more extreme long-range requirements of the coming American bombing campaign against Japan, the length of the missions and the very high fatigue factor anticipated for the escort pilots, interest in developing a twin-engined plane for the role was revived.

The development of the Twin Mustang came as the propeller-driven fighter era was ending. With the advent of the new jet fighters and their greatly superior performance, and the atomic bombing of Hiroshima and Nagasaki bringing the war to an end, everything changed. All remaining warplane contracts with American aircraft builders were cancelled. The peace dividend was at hand and very little funding was available for aircraft development. Everyone wanted to forget the war and all thought of new equipment for war.

It came as a huge shock to American military planners, when, during the 1947 Soviet Aviation Day at Tushino, three Tu-4 long-range strategic bombers, exact copies of the big Boeing B-29s interned by the Soviets during the war, appeared over the spectators. U.S. Intelligence knew that the USSR would soon have nuclear weapons and the Americans now knew too that, with the availability of the Tu-4, the U.S. would soon become vulnerable to Soviet nuclear attack. In an interim period during which new jet interceptors were being developed to counter such a threat, the existing Twin Mustangs were pressed into service with the United States Strategic Air Command, to be used as fighter escorts and all-weather air defense interceptors for the bombers of SAC. The first F-82s began operations with SAC at Kearney Air Force Base, Nebraska, in March 1948 with the 27th Fighter Escort Wing.

The mission of the 27th was escort the B-29s, B-50s, or Convair B-36 bombers of SAC on their very long-range missions to the Soviet Union, extremely lengthy flights from bases in Europe or Alaska. In the period between 1948 and the early

1950s, the F-82s were the only operational American fighters capable of shepherding the big bombers on a mission from, say, England to Moscow and back, with a loiter time over the target area of thirty minutes. The Twin Mustang's service ceiling of 40,000 feet allowed it to stay with the bombers and meet its mission requirement.

With the establishment of the Berlin Airlift and heightened tensions with the Soviets in 1948, the F-82s of the 27th FEW were deployed to McChord Air Force Base, Washington, and put on alert should hostilities break out in Europe. While at McChord, some of their number were detached for temporary duty with the 449th (All-Weather) Fighter Squadron in Alaska, which also flew the Twin Mustang. The pilots of the 27th briefly provided some transition training for the pilots of the 449th before returning to Washington.

The all-weather credentials of the F-82 were certainly confirmed in January of 1949 when the planes of the 27th were ordered to participate in a flypast at Carswell AFB, Fort Worth, Texas, along with many of SACs bomber fleet aircraft. The weather on that particular day was less than ideal. Blizzards raged throughout the Midwest and most major airports were closed. At Kearney AFB, home base to the 27th, the field was completely socked in by blizzard conditions, but still, an early briefing was held for the crews and the planes were readied for the flight to Texas. Runways and taxiways were cleared of the mounting snow and, at the appointed hour the F-82s got airborne and managed a rendezvous with the bombers. The flypast came off as planned and all present were mightily impressed with the performance of the Twin Mustangs in the vilest of weather.

As a part of military budget cutting, the Kearney base was closed in March 1949 and the 27th relocated to Bergstrom AFB, Texas. There, the unit began transitioning into the Republic F-84 Thunderjet and the old F-82s were phased out

of active service by September 1950. Most were sent to reclamation, probably to the "airplane graveyard" at Davis-Monthan
AFB near Tucson, Arizona. Some, however, went to combat in
the Korean War.

The war in Korea broke out on June 25th 1950 when more
than 75,000 troops of the North Korean People's Army began
a march south across the 38th parallel into the pro-Western
Republic of Korea in the initial military action of the Cold War
era. American troops soon entered the conflict on the side of
South Korea. U.S. President Harry Truman said at the time: "If
we let Korea down, the Soviets will keep right on going and
swallow up one place after another.

In the skies over Korea that summer, everything changed.
The technology of the 1940s was instantly replaced by a genuine game changer. Swept-wing jet fighters, the Soviet MiG-15
and the American F-86, outstripped the best of the propeller-
era fighters, along with the first fighters of the jet age, the
straight-winged Republic F-84, Gloster Meteor, and Lockheed
F-80. The biggest, best and most sophisticated bomber of the
prop-era, the 300-mile-an-hour B-29 too was no longer viable
in a time when the opposition could flash by at roughly twice
that speed. Either lead, follow, or get out of the way . . . those
were the options then for everything in the air that wasn't a
swept-wing jet.

The F-82 air crews on alert at Itazuke Air Base, Japan, in the
evening of June 24-25 learned at four in the morning that
ground forces of North Korea had invaded their neighbour
across the 38th parallel. They were immediately ordered on a
reconnaissance mission to report on road and rail activity
along the invasion route. They arrived in the area to find it
engulfed in cloud cover topped at 8,000 feet. Emerging from
the cloud at about 2,000 feet, the Twin Mustangs set course
toward Kimpo air base near Seoul in South Korea. En route

they spotted great convoys of military vehicles, trucks, and more than fifty tanks heading south. Having completed the recce, the F-82 pilots returned to Japan and a debriefing by staff from General Douglas MacArthur's headquarters, thus completing the first recorded combat mission of the Korean air war. The intelligence gathered in the flight confirmed the scale of the North Korean invasion force.

From a total of thirty-two Twin Mustangs in the Far East Air Force inventory, twenty-seven were made available by June 27th for use in Korea and they were formed into the 347th Provisional Fighter Group. Before dawn that same day they were airborne providing fighter cover for C-54 Skymaster transport planes carrying civilians out of the country to safety. The mission had been mounted due to concern that fighters of the North Korean Air Force might appear at the Kimpo airfield to shoot down the arriving and departing C-54s. One of the transports had been destroyed on the ground at Kimpo on June 25th by the North Koreans.

The F-82s circled over Kimpo airfield in three flights. At just before noon an assortment of Soviet-built Yak-9s, Yak-11s, and La-7s arrived in the area. A Yak-11 immediately attacked the F-82 of Lt. Charles Moran, damaging one of this vertical stabilizers. The Yak was then set upon by Lt. William Hudson in another of the Twin Mustangs who was able to get in firing position behind the Yak fighter after pulling a high-g turn. His machine-gun rounds struck the North Korean plane, which banked hard right to evade the American. Hudson's second burst holed the right wing of the Yak, destroying the flap and aileron and setting fire to a fuel tank. The damage prompted the North Korean pilot to bale out, but his observer, who was either dead or badly wounded, went down with the crippled aircraft. The enemy pilot landed on the Kimpo airfield and was surrounded by troops of the South Korean army. He drew his pistol and began firing at the soldiers who quickly returned fire, killing him.

Other F-82 pilots in the area of Kimpo engaged and destroyed two of the La-7s, allowing only two of the enemy aircraft to return to their base that day. The C-54 evacuation operations continued and Lt. Hudson was credited with the first aerial victory of the Korean War.

In that strange, uncertain period between the beginning of hostilities on the Korean peninsula and the arrival and availability of jet interceptors to take over the roles assigned to the F-82s there, the U.S. Air Force faced a serious operational problem. Production of the F-82 Twin Mustang had ceased in April 1948 and no one had planned for the provision of an appropriate supply of spare parts for the small fleet as it had only been built for an interim use and was not intended to remain in service after the new jets came on stream. The entire F-82 inventory amounted to only 182 aircraft and most of them were committed to operational units in the Pacific Northwest, Alaska, and the U.S. east coast. The air force needed the Twin Mustangs immediately to escort B-26 Invader bombers on their raids deep into North Korea, as well as for recce flights in search of ground targets on the Han River. Ground maintenance crews had no alternative to cannibalizing some of their F-82s to keep others airworthy. And the level of activity was high in that week following June 26th 1950, with the planes flying thirty-five sorties that averaged five hours each. The wear and tear on them was considerable.

Some of the pressure on the F-82 crews was relieved in July when some newly arrived Lockheed F-80 Shooting Star jets were able to stifle the progress of the North Korean Air Force in its attempted strikes below the 38th parallel. This enabled the F-82s to fly more escort missions as well as many night intruder missions. In these latter efforts, however, the planes suffered a number of hits, mainly ground fire, in their large, underslung radar radomes. Replacement radomes and radar units were then difficult to access and the ground crews were forced to remove the units, relegating the planes to a day-fighter role. As ground-support aircraft, the Twin Mustangs were most effective, bringing their 4,000-pound bomb and ordnance loads anywhere in the war zone. They also made good use of their six .50 calibre machine-guns against the many ground targets they found.

4th and 68th Squadron F-82s formed part of a major air strike on July 10th against North Korean road traffic of tanks, trucks and personnel carriers, as well as many enemy troops. The bombing objective of the escorted B-26s was an important river bridge whose destruction resulted in an impressive traffic jam for the North Koreans.

Ground support was a vital service being provided by the pilots of the Twin Mustangs throughout July and August. Some 68th Squadron F-82s were patrolling over South Korea during the night of August 27th when their leader received an urgent call for air support from a unit of United Nations ground troops pinned down by concentrated enemy mortar fire. After making initial passes to coordinate their attack with a ground controller, the American pilots spent the next forty-five minutes shooting up the enemy positions, silencing the mortar opposition and killing more than 300 of the North Korean troops.

From October, the use of the Twin Mustangs in Korea was shifted to flying early morning weather recce missions, along with an airfield alert readiness in the Seoul area. Now the bulk of the ground attack missions were being undertaken by F-51 Mustangs, F-80 Shooting Stars, and F-84 Thunderjets.

The situation changed again in December as large units of the Chinese Communist army entered the conflict in support of the North Koreans. Most of the F-82s were then committed to flying armed reconnaissance missions over southern North Korea, checking road activity by the Chinese. Their role was altered again in late January when they were ordered to fly continuous combat air patrols over the main airfields in the area of Pyongyang to monitor Chinese aircraft operations which were threatening the UN front lines.

The earlier operations of the F-82s had put the air and ground crews under considerable stress and strain. By mid-summer, though, the liklihood of the planes becoming involved in air-to-air combat had been significantly reduced, largely due to the increasing participation of the F-80s, F-84s, and the F-51 Mustangs, all of whom had become effective in preventing the aircraft of the North Korean Air Force from flying below the 38th parallel.

The use of the F-82 twin-Mustangs in escorting the B-26 missions to targets deep into North Korea brought their substantial and effective firepower in the form of their six .50-caliber machine guns with 400 rounds each and a 4,000-pound ordnance capability into play against the many ground targets available to them. The trips were not without hazard, however, as the F-82s, operating with droppable external fuel tanks, had to frequently drop these tanks due to the risk of fire or explosion should the tanks be hit by enemy ground fire.

By early July the 339th Squadron had been withdrawn from combat operations and reassigned to Johnson Air Base on the island of Okinawa. This was followed by the return of the 4th Squadron to Okinawa, the inactivation of the 347th Provisional Group, and control of the 68th Squadron being assigned to the Eighth Fighter Group. The 339th Squadron had been in combat for just ten days in late June and early July, flying a total of only forty-four combat sorties, actions for which they had been given no training. Throughout July and August, the F-82s of the 68th were required to carry on the battle, attacking enemy trains, vehicles, buildings, and strafing North Korean troops on the roads.

Time was running out for the Twin Mustangs in Korea by August 1951. By the end of the month, only eight of the planes remained operational in Korea as the new Lockheed F-94 Starfire all-weather interceptor was arriving in quantity and assuming much of the responsibilities formerly carried by the F-82s. And by April 1952, all such assignments were being flown by the F-94s. During their Korean War involvement, the Twin Mustangs had accounted for twenty enemy aircraft destroyed, four in the air and sixteen on the ground.

Several of the surviving F-82 Twin Mustangs were reassigned to a cold weather air defence role in Alaska, a mission they were well suited for with their long-range mission capability. There they patrolled the area in a time when the Soviets were regularly flying missions from Siberian airfields to test the air defences of the U.S. in that part of the world. Tensions were high there during and after the Korean War, and the job of responding to the constant testing and threats was shared by the F-82s with F-94 jets which, while much faster, had a far shorter range capability. Most of the F-82s were operated from Ladd AFB near Fairbanks, and from Adak Island.

By the time they arrived in Alaska, most of the Twin Mustangs that had served in Korea were in a badly run-down condition, many of them suffering serious corrosion and, of course, the continuing parts shortage which made maintenance difficult to almost impossible. Some limited long-range recce flying was carried out over the Bering Sea, but it was necessary to bring along an experienced flight mechanic in the right side cockpit to be on hand when the demands of these extremely long flights on the relatively high-time airplanes forced them to make emergency landings in remote and desolate locations. In such instances, the mechanic was normally able to make adequate repairs so the pilot could bring the aircraft back to the

Ladd base.

Finally, the shortage of spare parts, and ordinary attrition brought about the ultimate withdrawal of the last operational F-82s, roughly half of which had long since become "hangar queens", robbed of their precious parts to keep the others in the air. As fewer and fewer the of old machines were capable of being repaired by spring 1953, only a handful remained operational. Most of the planes were declared to be surplus to requirements, put in storage and eventually sent for reclamation and ending up in smelters for recovery of their metal as ingots. Four of the old F-82s were acquired by the National Advisory Committee for Aeronautics (NACA) where they served briefly in research work.

Five examples of the F-82 Twin Mustang are known to still exist. One was for many years a 'gate guardian' at Lackland AFB in Texas. It was ultimately acquired by what used to be called the Confederate Air Force, and is now known as the Commemorative Air Force. It was restored to flying condition and operated by the Texas organization until a landing accident in 1987. The plane could be repaired but locating the required replacement propellers and landing gear proved all but insurmountable. In 2009 the aircraft was returned to the U.S. Air Force (the National Museum of the U.S. Air Force, in Ohio) which had loaned it to the CAF originally. The museum staff have since restored it, repainted and marked it to replicate the aircraft that was flown by Lt. Charles Moran, in which he downed a North Korean La-7 on June 27th 1950 near the Kimpo Air Base in Korea.

A second Twin Mustang example survives on display in the Air Force Museum. It is shown in the markings it wore during an historic flight from Hawaii to New York in February 1947. The aircraft, named *Betty Jo*, made the 4,968-mile trip in fourteen hours and thirty-two minutes at an average speed of 342 mph with Colonel Robert E. Thacker at the controls. The plane carried a combined internal and external fuel load of 2,215 gallons. The achievement remains the longest nonstop flight ever made by a propeller-driven fighter plane. *Betty Jo* was an F-82B powered by Rolls-Royce Merlin engines. It has been in place at the Air Force Museum since June 1957.

Next on the short survivor list of Twin Mustangs is one of the two prototypes, the XP-82 number 44-83887. Aircraft restorer Tom Reilly of Douglas, Georgia, acquired the remains (a single left-side fuselage and some parts) of this historic aircraft in March 2008. For many years it had lain on the farm of airplane collector Walter Soplata, near Newbury, Ohio. Reilly intends to build a new right-side fuselage and rebuild the entire plane to flying condition.

Another airframe that had been a part of the Soplata collection in Ohio is an F-82E which has been sold to C&P Aviation of Anoka, Minnesota, which is restoring it to flying condition.

The last of the remaining Twin Mustangs, an F-82E, is a current gate guardian at Lackland AFB, Texas, and part of the USAF History and Traditions Museum of San Antonio, Texas.

KOREA

Lt A.E. Helseth, a young American U.S. Air Force pilot with barely 200 hours of Mustang flight time in his logbook, was flying in a section of Republic of Korea Air Force F-51s led by Major Dean Hess on the afternoon of July 10th 1950. Lt. Helseth was one of a group of American volunteer pilots serving with the ROKAF in the early days of the Korean War. The small force was heading for Chonan when Helseth realized that his radio was not working. At the same moment he happened to spot two North Korean tanks on a road below and tried without success to attract the attention of the others in his flight. He then broke away from the formation, dove and attacked one of the tanks.

After putting his target out of action, he became lost and looked around for a landmark he recognized. Instead, he found and proceeded to shoot up nine trucks and a half-track as he followed the road south. Still lost, and rapidly running out of fuel, Helseth chose to belly-land the Mustang before lack of fuel would force him down. As he approached the town of Haedong, he spotted what appeared to be a park and safely set the fighter down on the grass. That had been the easy part of the mission. Walking and hitchhiking back to his base at Taegu took him the next five days.

Spearheaded by masses of Russian-built T-34 tanks, units of the North Korean army rolled across the 38th parallel in an assault against Kaesong and Chunchon in South Korea on the morning of Sunday, June 25th 1950. As the Japanese had done less than a decade earlier at Pearl Harbor, Hawaii, the North Koreans chose to attack on a Sunday morning, when any response or resistance was likely to be minimal.

The Second World War had ended less than five years before this outbreak of new hostilities in Asia. On that June

Sunday, 897 F-51 and thirty-eight RF-51 Mustang fighters remained in the U.S. Air Force active inventory. A further 764 Mustangs were then being operated by the U.S. Air National Guard. The F-51Ds had sufficient supplies of spare parts, so they were chosen to go back to war and again, as in 1942, they went in a close-support role.

The first Mustangs to enter combat in the Korean Conflict, as it was then known, were the F-82 Twin Mustangs of the 68th and 339th All-Weather Fighter Squadrons. Ed Schmued: "Many people think the F-82 is nothing but two P-51 fuse-lages joined together by the wing. This is not the case. It was a completely new design. Nothing of the P-51, except the design principles and powerplant group, was used on this new venture. All the things that were good on the P-51 were also applied here. We developed designs of a low-cost train-er, low-cost fighter, and of a twin-fuselage fighter. We built a mock-up to find out if the off-center position of the pilot in a rapid roll would affect the two crewmen in any way. We found that there was no effect whatsoever. The pilot always had the feeling that the ship was rotating around his own fuselage."

On June 27th, F-82s shot down three enemy Yak-9 fight-ers, in the first Korean air combat action by the Americans. On the 29th, ten F-51Ds were assigned to protect Suwon Airfield, where General Douglas MacArthur was arriving to take command of the defense of South Korea. The Mustangs were led by Dean Hess and, as MacArthur watched, four enemy planes attacked the airfield and were all shot down by the American fighters.

U.S. President Harry Truman directed in late June that the American 5th Air Force achieve air superiority, isolate the battlefield through interdiction, and provide close air sup-port for the ground forces. Getting qualified Mustang pilots to Korea, however, was proving a bigger problem than getting Mustangs there.

By July F-51D Mustangs of the US Air Force from Japan, from the Royal Australian Air Force and from the South African Air Force, were all operating in Korea on tactical reconnaissance and ground support tasks. Collectively, they accounted for the downing of nineteen enemy propeller-driven planes and twenty-eight enemy aircraft on the ground. In July the Mustangs based at Taegu and Po'hang carried the load for the Allied forces in those early days of the conflict.

In the early months of the Korean War, accidents and mechanical troubles were responsible for several Mustang losses among the ROKAF units. In late December two such events occurred. Lt James Gillespie suffered engine failure and had to bail out of his F-51 near the front lines. An American infantry patrol located him and got him back to his base within two days. In another incident that week, Captain George Metcalf experienced engine trouble that same week while taking off from his base at Taejon and crash-landed near the end of the runway, injuring his back and suffering facial cuts. Both of these incidents resulted from fuel con-tamination, water in the fuel lines.

Only two days later Metcalf was flying an armed reconnais-sance mission when his flight was asked to provide cover for the rescue of a downed pilot. The Mustangs came under heavy anti-aircraft fire as they dove to strafe enemy soldiers near the location of the friendly pilot. The soldiers were attempting to reach and capture the pilot and, as Metcalf pulled up from a strafing pass, ground fire struck his F-51, blasting nearly three feet from the leading edge of one wing and damaging one aileron. Firmly bracing himself against the cockpit structure, he had to keep unremitting pressure on th stick and rudder to hold the Mustang in a controlled flight attitude. When the airspeed of the damaged fighter fell to near 250 mph, Metcalf felt the plane approaching a stall. He was forced to land the aircraft at high speed to maintain directional control, but brought it in safely.

Not all of the hazards faced by Mustang pilots in Korea were mechanical or directly combat-related. In the colder months especially, they had to contend with icing at relatively low altitudes from which recovery was nearly always impossible when the over-loaded aeroplane entered a stall or spin. Their Mustangs were not equipped with deicing systems and accumulating wing ice was a virtual death sentence for the pilots flying these ground support missions in winter. In addition to the threats they met in the air, the Mustang pilots had to cope with more mundane, but equally challenging situations on the ground. Shelter and living conditions on their bases were primitive and miserable. The brutal cold of the Korean winter caused a few airmen to rig some less than reliable heating arrangements involving oil and 100 octane aviation gas, and resulting in some serious fires, explosions and loss of life.

335 F-51D Mustangs were lost in the Korean War, with 264 pilots killed or missing. Of these losses, 172 fell to enemy ground fire, ten to enemy jet fighters, with forty-four missing and unaccounted for, and the remainder to accidents. Ed Schmued: "Unfortunately, the P-51 was a high-altitude fighter. [In Korea] it was used in ground support work, which is absolutely hopeless, because a .30-caliber bullet can rip a hole in the radiator and you fly two more minutes before your engine freezes up. Flying a P-51 in ground support was almost a suicide mission. It is unfortunate that the airplane had been used for ground support, but in the Korean conflict we were short of airplanes and anything had to do. This was the reason for using the P-51 in low-level operations."

Pilots of the Royal Australian Air Force flew Mustangs in Korea as a part of the United Nations force there and on September 9th 1950, RAAF 77 Squadron Flt. Lt. Roscoe

Coburn was attacking a target at Kigye, using rockets, when his F-51 was struck in the cooling system by ground fire. Coburn and his mates were operating from a base in Japan called Iwakuni and he headed back for it, accompanied by Flt. Lt. Jack Murry. As the two pilots flew across the Strait of Tsushima, the serious damage to Coburn's plane worsened. Streaming glycol coolant fumes were seeping into his cockpit and condensing on his canopy, eliminating his side vision and forcing him to begin flying on instruments. Soon Murry saw glycol streaming from Coburn's radiator shutter.

As the pair approached the Honshu coast, Coburn's engine temperature redlined and the Merlin started running roughly. Sparks began trailing from the engine exhaust stacks and Coburn knew he had only seconds to bail out. He quickly trimmed the aeroplane for hands-off flight so he could leave it. At that point the engine seized. The action caused the big four-blade prop to shear off and go spinning into space. For a brief period the Mustang continued on in a fairly steady glide while the loose prop spun slowly ahead and then downward towards the sea.

Ross Coburn bailed out as the plane crossed the coast and was soon in the hands of some Japanese farmers who escorted him to his base. Jack Murry was relieved to find Coburn safely back at Iwakuni later. He had not seen Coburn bail out, as he had been following the descent of the wayward propeller at the instant Coburn exited his Mustang.

Early in October, 77 Squadron was relocated to a field designated as K-3 at Po'hang in South Korea, cutting more than 300 miles off the lengthy combat missions of the unit. The living conditions at K-3 were considerably poorer than the pilots had been used to at Iwakuni. In Korea they now lived in drafty, flimsy, uncomfortable tents and were dependent for both heat and lighting on napalm burning in tin cans. The tough Aussies had not lived in cold like the approaching

Korean winter and were particularly miserable at night when the temperature dropped dramatically. They soon requested and were given American Air Force clothing, which proved far more useful in the conditions than their own uniforms.

In November the squadron was again relocated, this time to the Yongpo airfield near Hamhung, K-27, closer to their targets. With the move came the full force of Korean winter. However, Yongpo had been built by the Japanese during the Second World War and the Australians enjoyed the relative comforts of life in their permanent brick and stone buildings. Still, they suffered in the plummeting temperatures and heavy snows of the isolated base there on the coastal plain. It was worse for the ground crews toiling, in the zero daytime temperature and -20 degrees at night. The pilots shared some of the chores with their mechanics, sweeping accumulated snow from their planes, and helping with the arming and fueling.

The daily routine that winter had the Aussie pilots taking off at dawn to strike at enemy targets forty miles away near Chang Jin. They would return quickly to Yongpo to rearm and refuel before continuing the shuttle missions in support of U.S. Marines, until nightfall. Moving day came again on December 3rd when the men of 77 Squadron were required to take their Mustang fighter-bombers south to K-9, at Pusan, where the living standard was somewhat lower than that at Yongpo, but certainly better than the tents of Po'hang. Now they were quartered in wooden huts with concrete floors and gasoline-stove heating.

Operating from K-9, however, posed some special problems for the 77 Squadron pilots. With menacing, rocky hills on three sides of the field, and the western channel of the Korean Straight on the fourth side, prevailing winds required the Aussies to take off in their heavily-loaded F-51s towards the hills, with the corresponding danger, and to make their landing approaches over the sea, frequently causing depth perception disorientation. The other major problem in operating from K-9 was thick dust, clouds of it that found its way into their eyes, food, clothing, and their Mustangs. Vital equipment was affected; radio tuners were jammed, air filters clogged, and fuel contaminated.

In January, the pilots of 77 were assigned to bomb the Chinese Army Headquarters at Pyongyang, known to be the most heavily defended target in North Korea. The plan called for two flights of six Mustangs each, with one bringing bombs and the other napalm. Each Mustang was also carrying four rockets. The bomb-carrying '51s were to attack the target first and then use their rockets to suppress enemy anti-aircraft fire. The second flight would then strike with its napalm. The mission would test the maximum range of the Mustangs.

The first flight arrived as scheduled and dropped their bombs, but the second flight was delayed by deteriorating weather, arriving late over the target area. Their lateness found them dropping their napalm in the midst of a rain of bombs from several B-29s above them.

Austrailian Flt. Lt. Gordon Harvey's Mustang was damaged as he bore in on his napalm attack. One of his weapons was trailing a streak of the jellied compound as he continued his run. He then reported that his engine was losing power and he was going to try to belly-land along the edge of the Taedong River. He managed to put the plane down successfully and was observed running to hide in a haystack. His fellow pilots circled in a rescue protection effort, but little hope was held out for Harvey, who had come down 150 miles into enemy territory. The next day a rescue helicopter arrived in the area where Harvey had landed, but found only his wrecked Mustang and some footprints in the snow. In 1951 the North Koreans released a list of prisoners of war they were holding and Harvey's name appeared on it. On August 29th 1953, he was released from captivity.

In the nine months of their combat operations in Korea, 77 Squadron flew more than 3,800 combat sorties. They lost ten pilots in combat, two in a fire at Po'hang, two in accidents, and one who became a prisoner of war.

Major Louis Sebille commanded the 67th Fighter Squadron, USAF, and was leading a four-Mustang section out of Ashiya air base, Japan, on August 5th 1950, to provide close air support for a UN operation near Pusan, Korea. His planes carried two 500-pound bombs and four rockets each.

As they crossed the Sea of Japan, one of the F-51 pilots radioed Sebille that he was having a mechanical problem and was returning to Ashiya. The other three fighter-bombers continued on course towards Pusan. There they were redirected by a ground controller to Hamchang at a point on the Naktong river where North Korean troops were crossing. Many of these troops were on a sand bar in the middle of the river when Sebille attacked them. He released his bombs, but one of them would not dislodge. With the hung-up bomb still attached to his wing, he joined the other two Mustangs as they strafed enemy vehicles that were partially concealed under trees on the western river bank.

Circling in their rocket attacks on the vehicles, the '51s were exposed to small arms fire and Sebille's plane was struck in the radiator, which then began bleeding glycol. One of the other Mustang pilots, Captain Martin Johnson, radioed Sebille to warn him of the coolant loss. At first, there was no reply or acknowledgment from the Major. Then Johnson heard his commander say, "They hit me." Johnson suggested that Sebille head south-east for the UN base near Taegu, but the Major rejected the suggestion and said that he was going to "get that bastard." Johnson watched as Sebille's Mustang descended towards the target, guns blazing. He was shocked by the immense explosion as Sebille's plane, and its remaining bomb and rockets, detonated on contact with the enemy vehicle. Major Sebille was the first of four U.S. Air Force men to be awarded the Congressional Medal of Honor for his actions during the Korean conflict, and the last Mustang pilot recipient of the award.

FOURTH BUT FIRST

Grover C. Hall, Jr. served as Public Relations Officer of the famous 4th Fighter Group, 8th USAAF at Debden, England, in World War Two. There he got to know the storied pilots of the highest-scoring American fighter group in the European Theater of Operations. After the war he became editor-in-chief of the *Montgomery* [Alabama] *Advertiser*. The accounts in this chapter are based on his perspectives from his days at Debden.

As has already been recounted in the chapter *Blakeslee's Deal*, Colonel Don Blakeslee campaigned long and hard to get the 4th re-equipped with Mustangs after many months of flying combat missions in the P-47 Thunderbolt, a fighter that had not endeared itself to the colonel. He knew that, in the Mustang, his boys would have the means to successfully protect the heavy bombers of the Eighth Air Force all the way to the most distant targets and back. The plane was the best of the best and he was absolutely determined that his group would fly and fight it.

The story goes that way back in 1934, what would become the Debden aerodrome was an Essex farm about fifteen miles southeast of Cambridge, that belonged to a Mr A. C. Kettley. Kettley and his ancestors had farmed the land for more than eighty years, specializing in mainly in sugar beets and wheat, and growing them with great pride and enthusiasm. He fully expected that he would keep on growing them long into the future, as would his descendants.

Then one early evening in May his life changed. A Bristol Bulldog fighter fighter plane roared in low over the Kettley home, its engine coughing and sputtering. Clearly, the pilot had a problem with the machine and needed to land in a hurry.

One of Kettley's wheat fields appeared beneath the wing of the Bulldog and the pilot decided it was as good a place as any to set down. Gliding low over the farmer's head, the RAF airman gently ploughed a new, deep and unwelcome furrow in the wheat. At the end of its short run, the plane nosed over and buried its prop and spinner in the rich dark soil. "What are you doing in my wheat field?," barked Kettley. Taking stock of the situation, the pilot noted that he was still alive as the farmer repeated his question with considerable impatience. "Your wheat, huh," replied the pilot. "If it hadn't been for your blasted wheat, my bus wouldn't have overturned!" Then, relaxing a bit, he said to the farmer, "Sir, let's off to the nearest pub. My treat and pleasure." Kettley accepted the invitation after first draining the remaining six gallons of petrol from the Bulldog.

The next day Air Ministry officials arrived to investigate the mishap and while there examined the soil in the wheat field. "Wonderful land," they observed. Shortly thereafter a party of RAF officers arrived and greeted the farmer with "Kettley, we've got good news for you—we've come to buy your farm for an airdrome site." "To hell with you!" bellowed Mr Kettley. In the end, though, with the nation and the air force preparing for a virtually inevitable war, A.C. Kettley had no choice and was forced to sell.

With the construction and establishment of the airdrome came a succession of airmen of different stripes. First to arrive were the RAF, followed soon after by a contingent of Free Poles. Grover Hall: "Finally, came a third set of tenants who wore pink pants and forest green tunics to the amazement of the English. The Americans talked louder than the others, stayed gone much longer when they took off for the day's work across the Channel, and painted bulgy nudes and such-like on their planes. Sometimes the Americans rented rooms in the Kettley domicile so their wives could visit them on weekends.

Mrs Kettley, an unworldly little lady, was sometimes perplexed that the appearance of the wives of the officers seemed to change so radically from visit to visit."

The new Debden base served as a key operational fighter station during the Battle of Britain and the Blitz. The first shot by an RAF fighter in the Battle was supposedly fired by a Hurricane flying from the base. When the Germans switched their attentions from Channel convoys and radar targets to the fighter fields of the Royal Air Force in mid-August 1940, Debden was among the field visited by the enemy bombers on a Saturday morning. Bombs fell on the east/west runway and the repairs left a permanent hump in it. Farmer Kettley later recalled his own memory of the morning raid: "I lost two cows, three calves, seven hogs, 56 head of poultry, including two geese, and my two swans flew away and never came back."

The desperate pilot shortage in the RAF of 1940 caused it to be receptive to the likes of what became known as the Eagle Squadrons, units of American young men volunteering to fly and fight with their RAF while wearing an "E.S." flash on their sleeves. Their presence was very well received in the pubs, in buses and taxis, and on the streets of Britain in that period, perhaps making some Britons feel a bit less alone in their country's stance against the German enemy. The Eagles helped to, in Churchill's words, ". . . Carry on the struggle, until, in God's good time, the New World, with all its power and might, steps forth to the rescue and liberation of the Old." But they were a strange, mixed lot of the good and not so good, in it for the duration.

The Eagles flew Spitfire Vs and Hurricanes and were just getting going by the end of the Battle of Britain, flying convoy patrols mostly and doing a lot of instructing. Of the three operational Eagle Squadrons, No 71 shared the Debden airfield with two other RAF squadrons. The first important fighting for the Eagles came with the Dieppe Raid in August 1942. In the action over the beaches, future names of note with the 4FG, Don Blakeslee, Don Gentile, and Chesley Peterson all got into it with bombers and fighters of the Luftwaffe, Blakeslee and Gentile each downing two. Peterson shot down one German fighter and was then shot down himself, bailing out and landing in the Channel. That night the Eagle pilots celebrated the events of the day at their favourite local, the White Heart in Saffron Walden, near the Debden base. The evening was capped off when the phone rang; it was Peterson announcing his rescue from the icy waters off Dieppe.

Another evening the Eagle pilots would long remember was that of the English premiere of a Hollywood movie about them, *Eagle Squadron*. They had heard about it and eagerly anticipated seeing it.

As author and film historian James Farmer wrote in *Celluloid Wings*, "Universal's *Eagle Squadron* was the first full-blown, American air-war film to be largely produced after Pearl Harbor. The opening moments get off to an excellent start. The film's documentary-style foreword, delivered with great solemnity by Quentin Reynolds, begins, 'This is the story of some our countrymen who did not wait to be stabbed in the back. These boys (of No 71 Eagle Squadron) . . . knew that the security of our country must depend upon our dominating and controlling the air.' Reynolds goes on to introduce a number of the unit's real-life pilots, including Battle of Britain veteran Eugene Tobin; Gregory 'Gus' Daymond, a former Hollywood makeup man who was then 'the acknowledged ace' of the squadron with six victories; C. W. McColpin, twelve victories by war's end; and the future No 71 Squadron Leader Chesley Peterson, who had seven victories. Chronologically, this opening scene must be set in early September 1941; it was in this month that McColpin first joined No 71 and Tobin, a former MGM studio guide and messenger boy, was killed on September 7, within days of his appearance for the cameras.

"Despite a great deal of excellent expository footage of Mark IIA and VB Spitfires from No 71, No 222, and possibly No 27 squadrons, this Walter Wanger production quickly degenerates into pure B-grade air pulp fiction.

"The members of the Eagle Squadrons invited to the London premiere of the film were "shocked at what they saw. American Eagle Lee Gover later recalled: 'The film was so far-fetched from actual combat . . . it was embarrassing.' The Eagles were special guests, sharing the theater with many distinguished Britons that evening. A mass walkout was impossible. But Gover, 'Mickie' Lambert, and a number of the other Eagles did in fact sneak down the side aisle and exit through a side door during the second half of the film.

"Bill Geiger, who is seen in the opening moments of the film, recalled: 'That movie upset everybody, and Squadron Leader Peterson in particular. We had been told that it would be a documentary, like the *March of Time* of those days. We all felt that we had been double-crossed. Pete was so bitter about it that he never responded to any requests for information or publicity about the Eagles from that day forward.' At this time, Peterson as commanding officer of the 71st was averaging a call 'a week' from correspondents and cameramen wanting to do a spread on the unit for some stateside magazine or newsreel agency. After the Universal film, even Quentin Reynolds, who remained a favorite with many of the Eagles, was refused access to the field by Peterson. Gover explained the Eagles' position. 'We were just another RAF squadron trying to do our best. We deserved, and wanted, no special attention—because of our American background—which overshadowed the British- (and Commonwealth) manned squadrons who were doing the same job and with whom we had to fly.' "

On September 29th 1942, the three Eagle Squadrons were all assembled at Debden, transferred from the RAF into the U.S.

Army Air Force and formed into the new 4th Fighter Group of the Eighth Air Force. In recognition of their prior service flying for the RAF, the former Eagles were entitled to wear their RAF wings on their new American air force tunics as well as the silver wings of USAAF pilots. Lined up on the parade ground under a steady drizzle, they listened as Air Chief Marshal Sir Charles Portal addressed them, "On the occasion of the merging of the Eagle Squadrons with the U.S. Air Corps, I would like to thank them for all they have done during the past two years. The RAF will never forget how the members of the Eagle Squadrons came spontaneously to this country, eager to help us in the critical weeks and months during and after the Battle of Britain.' "

When they considered the many differences between life as a fighter pilot in the RAF and in the USAAF in that war, the former Eagles saw considerable improvement in the food and the pay. The new American fighter group at Debden meant an end to Bubble and Squeak for breakfast, and, instead of the monthly pay of an RAF Pilot Officer of $76, they were now paid $276.

For a long time they had been used to, and comfortable flying the Mk V Spitfire, a fast, agile, highly effective British fighter with, it must be said, a relatively short range. They had roughly two years' experience of air combat operations in the ETO, some familiarity with the capabilities of the German Air Force, and a healthy respect for the demands and dangers of air fighting against their determined, skilled enemy.

Suddenly, they were hearing rumours that the group was soon to be re-equipped with a new, unproven fighter plane, the Republic P-47 Thunderbolt. This possibility met with almost universal disapproval as they dejectedly anticipated having to fly a new plane that was probably no better than some other American fighters like the P-39 and P-40, planes considered inadequate for the demands of combat in European skies.

The rumours were soon confirmed, but the pilots were given a reprieve of sorts. Until the delayed arrival of the Thunderbolts, they would continue to fly their Spitfires. But in March 1943, the day came when the pilots of the 4FG were to take their new planes into combat for the first time. Most of them missed the light, compact feeling of their Spitfires and disliked the great size, bulk and weight of the Thunderbolt. They thought that the glassed canopy and the mirror on the big plane would make it difficult to spot enemy planes, and many replaced the mirrors with Spitfire mirrors. They especially complained about the P-47's performance: "They won't climb; they won't turn tight, they won't do anything but dive."

While flying along the French coast on April 15th 1943, Don Blakeslee was in the lead of ten 4FG Thunderbolts. He spotted three Fw 190s at 30,000 feet and dove on them. He focused on one of the Germans and concentrated the fire of his eight .50 calibre guns, following the enemy plane down to 500 feet. The German pilot tried unsuccessfully to bail out and the wreck of the 190 splattered across the back garden of a house in Ostend. That night Blakeslee was congratulated on his victory and on showing how effectively the P-47 could dive in an attack. "It ought to dive," he said. "It certainly won't climb."

As good as the P-47 was, and it was a very good airplane indeed, like the Spitfire and the P-38 Lightning, it simply lacked the range to safely and effectively escort the heavy bombers of the Eighth to many German targets on the European continent.

On October 10th 1943, the Thunderbolts of the 4FG were assigned to protect the B-17 Flying Fortresses of the 390th Bomb Group on a bombing raid to a target at Munster, Germany. When the bombers neared the target area, they were too strung out for the fifty Thunderbolts to give them proper protection. Thirty+ German fighters appeared as the B-17s were turning onto their bomb run. The American fighters ripped into the approaching German planes, but before the battle could develop, Blakeslee, who was again leading the Debden pilots, was forced to order them to return to England as they were at the limit of their fuel range. He also had to make the familiar call to the bombers they were shepherding: "Horseback to Big Friends. Sorry. We'll have to leave you now." The bomber crews could only watch apprehensively as their precious fighter cover wheeled around for the haven of England. With accurate knowledge of when the USAAF escort fighters would have to turn back at the limit of their combat radius, the German fighter defenses immediately launched into a savage attack on the B-17s, shooting down ten of them in the next few frantic minutes.

Grover Hall: "A German rocket caught a Fort amidships. It broke in half and one half nosed up and collided with another Fort. A waist gunner was rocketed out of the flaming, splintered bomber in a grotesque swan dive four miles above Germany. His chest was shot away. In a short time some fifty aircraft, American and German alike, were burning and crashing to earth. But the majestic Forts—never once in the whole war were they turned back from a target—ground forward on their bomb runs. Still the Germans swarmed in with tempestuous acrobatics. The interiors of the bombers were splattered with blood whose clots froze in the icy blasts screaming through cannon and rocket rents.

"One of the first bombers knocked out of the sky was piloted by Lt John G. Winant, Jr., son of the U.S. ambassador to the Court of St. James.

"Another thirty-six fighters were sighted dead ahead, coming in for a bare-knuckle head-on attack. Bomber ammunition was all but exhausted, the floors were ankle deep in bullet hulls and wounded gunners bled in them, some dying of their wounds and others dying because they were too weak to connect themselves with oxygen.

"White vapor trails appeared to the west, but this time it wasn't enemy fighters. 'I felt like yelling and praying at the same time,' said a Fort pilot. It was a fresh group of Thunderbolts coming in as part of the relay escort. The German fighters disappeared.

"True, ten of the Forts had been able to destroy sixty German fighters, an amazing performance and far above the average. But eight of the ten Forts in this one box had been shot down—eighty men lost. Had the 4th's Thunderbolts not been forced to turn back for lack of fuel, they could have protected the bombers from this murderous attack. But the Germans had craftily waited for the interim during which the 4th turned back and the next escort relay was on the way. The Germans capitalized [on] this fighter weakness and there was talk that the United States would have to abandon daylight bombing the same as Germany and England had."

December 1943. The 354th Fighter Group, the pioneering group of the Ninth Air Force, arrived in England. Hall: "They were a great bunch of pilots, as they afterwards proved, but they needed someone to lead them on their first few missions to show them around. Blakeslee was the natural choice. He went over to the 354th base and led the group on several missions. But each night he flew back to Debden, pearl of the ETO, explaining that he couldn't bear the 354th's primitive Nissen hut station. But probably Blakeslee derived a malicious pleasure in seeing his pilots crowd about his borrowed Mustang, mouths watering, agog and enraptured with his enthusiastic account of the Mustang's capabilities. 'It's the ship,' Blakeslee said.

"Bended knee is not a military posture, but a little later Blakeslee was virtually genuflecting as he implored Major General Kepner, VIII Fighter Command Chief, to provide the 4th with Mustangs."

The 4th Fighter Group of World War Two was the highest-scoring American fighter organization in the ETO, with more than 1,000 enemy aircraft destroyed.

POSTWAR

In the years after the Second World War and the Korean conflict, many Mustangs were acquired by civilian enthusiasts, some for as little as $1,500. One such buyer was Albert Paul Mantz, the crack movie pilot. By 1946, Mantz had accumulated a collection of thirty-two aircraft of various types and ages which he used in film work for the Hollywood studios. He was about to expand considerably with the purchase of many surplus war planes.

An American organization called the Reconstruction Finance Corporation was disposing of thousands of fighters, bombers, trainers and transports at several locations around the U.S., one being Stillwater, Oklahoma, where the field, ramps, and runways were littered with hundreds of war-weary machines.

Mantz and his financial backers outbid their competition to become the owners of 500 military aircraft—eight Mustangs, seventy-five B-17 Flying Fortresses, 228 B-24 Liberators, ten B-25 Mitchells, twenty-two B-26 Marauders, ninety P-40 Warhawks, six P-39 Airacobras, thirty-one P-47 Thunderbolts and thirty miscellaneous types. He paid a total of $55,000. for the lot—not much considering the American government had paid $117,000,000. for them a few years before. Mantz knew too, that the aviation gas remaining in their tanks was worth more than his purchase price for the planes themselves. He believed that the scrap value of the aluminium alone was probably in excess of $150,000., and there was at least $100,000. worth of Plexiglas in them as well. But the deal came with a definite downside. Mantz was required by the government to remove all of his planes from the Stillwater site by a deadline date that he soon discovered he could not meet.

The logistics of moving that vast fleet of planes from mid-

America to Mantz's California base of operations proved insurmountable and, in a final, desperate effort to keep a small portion of his newly acquired air force, he turned to a long-time friend in the motion picture industry, asking a long-time friend, Bill Guthrie of Warner Brothers. Warners was known for making more aviation-related movies than any other filmmaker in that time and Mantz tried to persuade Guthrie that the studio would save a lot of money by establishing its own Aviation Department. He told the Warners man that if the studio would pay the cost of moving twelve of the aircraft to California for him, he would provide the planes for use in Warner Brothers movies for half the usual price. Guthrie, however, replied that he preferred to remain strictly in the movie business, not the junk business.

Mantz had to settle for bringing only twelve of the best aircraft in his purchase to Burbank Airport near Los Angeles on his own. He was forced to let his business partners sell the remainder of his warplane fleet for scrap.

Of the twelve aircraft Mantz kept, three would receive special attention. One was a promising B-25 Mitchell bomber that he rebuilt into a near-perfect aerial camera plane with an enlarged Plexiglas nose and a swiveling director's chair. He named it *The Smasher* and used it for many years to capture some of the most spectacular aerial cinematography ever made, footage for great films like *The Best Years of Our Lives*. The other two were P-51 Mustangs, which he revered. He had never flown a Mustang until one week before the 1946 Bendix Trophy Race, but within ten flight hours he declared himself ready to compete in the post-war resumption of the classic race from Los Angeles to Cleveland.

In the early morning of August 31st, the field of entrants lined up for the start was made up of ten P-38 Lightnings, four P-51 Mustangs, one Goodyear FG-1 Corsair, two Bell P-63 Kingcobras, and one Douglas A-26 Invader. Mantz had flown in three previous Bendix dashes and was a shrewd and high-ly-skilled competitor. His primary concern was whether his Mustang could outperform another Mustang in the field, the entry of aviatrix Jackie Cochran. Her aeroplane was a brand new factory-fresh example. He worried about that and about how he could carry enough fuel to average close to the 487 mph top speed his P-51 could achieve, without carrying drag-inducing drop tanks and without landing to refuel. He consulted another old friend about the problem, Lockheed's Kelly Johnson, who suggested plugging up the wings and filling them with fuel.

When people asked Mantz where he planned to land to refuel along the route, he told them truthfully that he was going to use 'wet wings.' Mantz and his team worked under wraps to prepare the P-51 in a hangar at Van Nuys airport in the San Fernando Valley north of Los Angeles. He had painted the plane a deep crimson and named it *Blaze of Noon*, after a film on which he had recently worked.

A slide rule and a banana were suspended from strings tied in the cockpit of his Mustang that morning. All the engines of the entrants were running and the first to depart for Cleveland was the Corsair. Several others followed and then it was the turn of *Blaze of Noon*. As the red Mustang thundered into the air, and Mantz raised the landing gear, the aircraft suddenly began to buffet severely and slowed dangerously near to stalling. Knowing that the gear had a sequencing problem, he debated for a moment whether to circle for several hours to burn off fuel before trying an emergency landing, or to try something else. He chose the latter and climbed to 25,000 feet over the town of Palmdale in the high desert northeast of Los Angeles.

Pulling through the top of a loop, he seemed to lose control of the aeroplane in a snapping manoeuvre that sprang the landing gear down. He tried retracting the wheels once more and this time the gear came up properly. He was then able to head off for Cleveland, re-plotting his course and settling in for the long ride.

His worry about Jackie Cochran's competition would be unwarranted. She came up against a 30,000-foot stack of thunderhead clouds over the Grand Canyon and tried to climb above the storm. Her engine quit as she ascended through 27,000 feet. She then headed down through the clouds flying on instruments at full speed. Some time later her problems were compounded when she jettisoned her drop tanks. The slip-stream knocked them into the trailing edges of her wings, damaging the wings significantly.

Mantz was also flying on instruments and flat out. As he crossed over the Mississippi River he started a long descent through more thunderstorms, and finally flashed over the Cleveland airport at 500 miles an hour to win the 1946 race and the $10,000 prize with an average speed of 435 mph. He entered and won the 1947 and 1948 Bendix Trophy Races as well—the only pilot ever to win the event in three consecutive years.

The revival of the American National Air Races after the Second World War resulted in many war-surplus P-51s being converted to greater and lesser racing configurations. The racing flourished until 1950 when the Korean War halted it again. It resumed in 1953 for five years as an entirely military event. There were no races from 1958 through 1960, but they were again resumed for two more years in 1961.

National Championship Air Racing began at Reno, Nevada, in 1965, opening a new era in racing for the Mustang, which dominated and continues to dominate that event.

The memorable, highly modified Mustang, Frank Taylor's P-51D 'Dago Red', appeared there and also achieved a new world's speed record. The 42-year-old 3,000-hp Packard

Merlin-equipped racer set a piston-engined aircraft mark of 517 mph.

For many years Robert A. 'Bob' Hoover served as the official starter of the Reno Air Races Unlimited Class events. The racing planes, mostly Mustangs, formed up each year line-abreast on Hoover's P-51D Old Yeller and, when he was sat-ified that they were properly ordered, he would announce to them and the crowd below, "Gentlemen, you have a race!" He would then pull up sharply to circle overhead, ready to man-age things in the event of an accident, while the competitors dove into the first turn.

For much of his career Bob Hoover flew as test/demonstration pilot for North American Aviation. Much of his time with the planemaker was spent impressing airshow crowds around the United States with what the Mustang could do in the hands of a truly exceptional airman. The 85-year-old now denies that he was born in a nest, but admits to having taught himself aerobatics when he learned to fly as a young-ster at Nashville's Berry Field before the war. He then joined the Tennessee National Guard and, after graduating from Army Pilot Training, was sent to England and on to North Africa.

Later, in Sicily, Hoover flew Spitfires with the 52nd Fighter Group and was shot down off the coast of southern France on his fifty-ninth mission. He spent the next sixteen months in the German prison camp Stalag Luft One at Barth on the Baltic near Stralsund. After the war Bob tested enemy aircraft for the Air Force at Wright Field, Ohio, and was hired by North American in 1950 to test their new jet fighters, the F-86 Sabre, FJ-2 Fury, and F-100 Super Sabre. He went to Korea during the war there to demonstrate the F-86 in dive-bombing missions. In more than fifty years of aviation, he has flown hun-dreds of aircraft types and performed thousands of spectacu-

asts. He is probably the best-known airshow pilot in the world and one of the most accomplished, high-achieving pilots in history. The late General Jimmy Doolittle, referred to Hoover as: ". . . the greatest stick and rudder man who ever lived."

In addition to the hundreds of Mustangs operated by U.S. Air National Guard and U.S.A.F. Reserve squadrons through the 1950s, more than 200 P-51Ds were built in Australia by the Commonwealth Aircraft Corporation near Melbourne after North American had ended its production. A further 300 were provided to Australia under a Lend-Lease agreement with the United States. Three Mustang-equipped squadrons were operated in Japan by the Australians as part of the Allied occupation after the Second World War. Additionally, the Royal Canadian Auxiliary Air Force ordered 130 Mustangs after the war for use into the 1950s and thirty were purchased by the Royal New Zealand Air Force in 1951.

The Chinese Nationalist Air Force received fifty P-51Ds prior to the Japanese surrender in August 1945, but some of them were captured by the Chinese Communists. Thirty other air forces that operated Mustangs after the war included those of Sweden, Cuba, Israel, the Dominican Republic, Egypt, Nicaragua, Haiti, Guatamala, Honduras, El Salvador, Bolivia, France, Italy, Switzerland, the Netherlands, Somalia, South Korea, and the Philippines.

In 1961, Trans-Florida Aviation Company of Sarasota, Florida, began a programme converting F-51D Mustangs to tandem two-seat executive aircraft. They called their product the Cavalier 2000 and tailored it for business types who wanted high-speed, long-range cruising coupled with the thrill of flight in a famous fighter plane. The Cavalier could subject its passenger to +9G at up to 490 mph with a cruise of 424 mph at 30,000 feet. It was equipped with twin 220-gallon wingtip fuel tanks for a 2,000-mile range and up to 400 pounds of luggage could be stored in what had been the wing gun bays. It was a relatively luxurious travel alternative for wealthy, and adventurous business types.

With American involvement in the Viet Nam war in the mid-1960s, the Cavalier people decided to offer a counterinsurgency version of their Mustang to the U.S. government. The 1,595-hp V-1650-7 Packard Merlin engine was replaced with a 1,760-hp British Merlin 620 and the aeroplane was made capable of carrying 4,000 pounds of underwing stores and, like the original P-51D, six .5 caliber machine guns in the wings. The P-51H taller tail fin was installed and the cockpit fitted with an ejection seat. By 1971, Trans-Florida had renamed itself Cavalier Aircraft Corporation and was producing a further advanced version of their Mustang called the Enforcer, a Lycoming turbine engined machine of 2,535 hp. None of these aircraft, however, were adopted by the U.S. Air Force.

By 1975, there were 148 P-51 Mustangs on the United States civil register, and several more in various stages of rebuilding and restoration. Massive gatherings of warbird aircraft at events such as the annual Experimental Aircraft Association meeting at Oshkosh, Wisconsin, attract dozens of Second World War planes, many of them Mustangs which continue to excite and inspire owners, pilots, and enthusiasts worldwide seven decades after their creation. Of the 15,875 Mustangs built, it is believed that upwards of 280 remain today with about 150 being airworthy.

The eighty-five-year-old Ed Schmued, the much admired and highly regarded designer of the Mustang, died in Oceanside, California, on June 1st 1985. An assemblage of aviation luminaries attended a memorial service two weeks later in the hangar of Clay Lacy Aviation at Van Nuys Airport, along with Ed's widow Christel, his daughter Sandra and son Rolf. When they learned of his request that his ashes be flown out to sea in a Mustang, his greatest creation, six P-51 owners offered their aeroplanes for the purpose, along with the owner of an F-86 Sabre, North American's jet successor to the Mustang. At the conclusion of the memorial service, a bugler played 'Taps' and the seven aircraft taxied slowly out to the runway with Lacy's purple P-51 in the lead.

In the air the little formation turned south towards Los Angeles International Airport where it made a single low-level pass over the site of the old North American Aviation plant where the Mustang had been created. It then headed directly out to sea where Ed's ashes were released as he had requested. Thirty minutes after they had taken off, the seven fighters were back on the ground at Van Nuys. The pilots on the flight were Clay Lacy, John Malone, Elmer Ward, Pete Regina, Skip Holm, Bob Guilford and Dave Zeuschel.

At the service it was mentioned that Ed's proudest achievement was the Mustang and how proud he was that it had contributed so much to ending the war in Europe and had been designed by a man born in Germany, powered by an engine designed in Britain, and built on American soil. Tributes arrived from powerful aviation personages, among them General James H. Doolittle: "All of us who had the good fortune to know—and to know was to admire—Edgar Schmued—miss him profoundly," and USAF General Chuck Yeager: "I, like a lot of other young fighter pilots, owe our necks to the design and performance that Ed put into that airplane [the P-51]. I was in the first P-51 group in the Eighth Air Force . . . the 357th Fighter Group. It was the best airplane in the skies anywhere in the world during WWII. Even during these days of high-tech airplanes, the P-51 Mustang is still a fun airplane to fly!"

KEEP 'EM FLYING

Someone once said "What we learn from history is that we don't learn from history." Well, yes and no. It is certainly true that when man ignores or dismisses the lessons of history, he may be condemned to repeat them. It is also true that when we purposefully set out to discover and understand aspects of our history, we gain some knowledge about why things were done as they were, what mistakes were made, what was done well, and what resulted.

One of the ways in which we learn about the Second World War and more recent conflicts is through the warbird movement. Warbird has become a standard reference for an aeroplane which was developed for the use of the military and is currently held in private (normally non-military) ownership. Enthusiasts and collectors have been acquiring such planes, mainly since the end of WWII, to preserve and, in many cases, fly them for the pleasure, entertainment, and education of the public through airshows and other displays.

The pace of the movement picked up dramatically in the 1960s with the filming and attendant publicity of the motion picture *Battle of Britain*—that, and the demise of the Soviet Union in 1991, which led to the discovery and acquisition of many wartime aircraft by aficionados in the west. The more history-minded among them have long felt that at least a few examples of the most important types of these aircraft should be saved, reprieved from the scrapman, and restored either to flying condition or pristine static display configuration. They have loved these old machines and wanted to celebrate them and show them to the general public and to young people in particular. They weren't out to glorify war but have sometimes been criticized for that.

The world centres for warbird activity are Chino in southern

California and Duxford, near Cambridge, England. At the start of the Second World War, Cal-Aero Academy operated an independent flying school at the Chino Airport in San Bernardino County. Cal-Aero was contracted by the U.S. Army Air Forces to give primary flight training to Army air cadets during the war years. It operated Boeing Stearman and Vultee BT-13 Valiant trainers. Schools like Cal-Aero were established in 1941 to provide the pilots then urgently needed by the Army. Cal-Aero closed in late 1944 when demand for primary flight training was lessening and the war had entered its final year.

At war's end Chino was one of several American locations used for the storage and disposition of thousands of military aircraft that had been returned from the war zones. The majority of these aeroplanes got the chop and, via portable field smelters, were turned into aluminium ingots destined to become pots, pans and other items less glamourous than fighters or bombers.

Two fine collections of warplanes are housed at Chino— Planes of Fame, and the Yanks Air Museum. Founded in the 1950s by Ed Maloney, Planes of Fame was the first permanent air museum west of the Rockies. It was initially located in Claremont, California, before its growth required a move to Ontario Airport, followed by a further move in 1973 to its present home at Chino. Maloney was among the first people to recognize the importance of preserving the aeroplanes of WWII, most of which were being sold off to recover their scrap metal.

In addition to its two aviation museums, the Chino airport facility is home to several companies that specialize in the restoration of warbirds, one being Fighter Rebuilders headed by Steve Hinton, one of the world's finest warbird pilots. Fighter Rebuilders is well known for its superb restorations for clients such as The Fighter Collection, Duxford, and the

Palm Springs Air Museum, in California. Hinton is famous too as a movie pilot, airshow performer and unlimited air racing champion. He is also president of the Planes of Fame Air Museum. Steve appears regularly at the Flying Legends airshow at Duxford in July.

The force behind Flying Legends, one of the world's great aviation events, is Stephen Grey of The Fighter Collection. TFC is one of the best collections of Second World War fighter aircraft, most of them flyers and many of them featured in Legends and the other annual Duxford displays. Among the most historically significant aeroplanes in the collection is *Twilight Tear*, a P-51D Mustang which was part of the 78th Fighter Group based at Duxford during WWII. *Twilight Tear* was flown by Lt. Hubert Davis of the 83rd FS, who shot down three enemy aircraft, two of which were Messerschmitt Me 262 jet fighters.

Another TFC fighter that has earned its place in history is the Grumman F6F Hellcat that was flown by U.S. Navy Lt. Alex Vraciu of VF-6, who downed six Japanese dive bombers in only eight minutes during the "Great Marianas Turkey Shoot" of June 19-20 1944. Lt. Vraciu has been credited with nineteen aerial victories in total.

In 2008, the great Flying Legends Air Display featured five P-51D Mustangs and one TF-51D Mustang, eleven Vickers-Supermarine Spitfires and one Seafire, a Hawker Hurricane and a Sea Hurricane, two Gloster Gladiators, one each Grumman Wildcat, Grumman Hellcat, and Bearcat, a Curtiss Hawk and two Curtiss Warhawks, a Yak-3 and a Yak-9, two Hawker Nimrods, two Boeing B-17s, a Piper L-4, a Douglas C-47 and a C-53, along with nineteen other types. It also marked the return to the air of AR213, then the world's only airworthy Mk 1a Spitfire.

In addition to The Fighter Collection, Duxford provides a base for other warbird preservation and restoration companies, including Historic Flying Limited, B-17 Preservation Ltd., Plane Sailing, The Old Flying Machine Company, and Aircraft Restoration Company. Other restoration/preservation/operators in the UK include the Battle of Britain Memorial Flight, Hardwick Warbirds, the Hangar Eleven Collection, Historic Aircraft Collection, the Real Aeroplane Company, the Royal Navy Historic Flight, the Shuttleworth Collection, Personal Plane Services, and the Woodchurch Warbirds.

The Old Flying Machine Company was established in 1981 by former RAF Red Arrows leader Ray Hanna and his son, Mark. For many years the Hannas, now both deceased, provided thrilling air displays and magnificent movie flying in the films *Memphis Belle*, *Empire of the Sun* (both of which featured Mustangs), *Dark Blue World*, and others.

The American Reconstruction Finance Corporation, and later the War Assets Administration, operated six large storage areas at airfields in the U.S. beginning in 1946—Kingman, Arizona; Walnut Ridge, Arkansas; Altus and Clinton, Oklahoma; Augusta, Georgia; and Ontario, California. In the beginning, storage and preservation was the primary function of these immense parking lots for the veteran warplanes. Through experimentation with a B-24 Liberator bomber, it was found that the thorough dismantling of such an aircraft to recover its 32,000 pounds of spare parts was extremely labour-intensive, requiring upwards of 800 man-hours. Policy was then changed; the engines and propellers, armament, radios and instruments were removed from all aircraft destined for salvaging. The airframe was then hacked into sections small enough to be easily fed into portable field smelters which melted the aluminium and the molten metal was then formed into ingots and sold to bidders.

Many sales were held to dispose of the aircraft, engines

and the spare parts. The aircraft that were considered non-saleable, for whatever reason, were destroyed.

By March 1946, 16,000 American ex-military aircraft were still overseas awaiting disposition. More than 9,000 of them were eventually flown back to the United States. More than 5,000 such aircraft sat in Germany and France—P-51s and P-47s at Furth, P-51s and P-38s at Fritzlar, L-4s and L-5s at Goppingen, P-47s at Hesich-Lictenau, B-17s at Holzkirchen, P-51s and P-47s at Kassel, and B-26s at Landsburg. Some 1,200 gliders were stored in France at Beauvais and Creil.

The non-saleable combat aircraft in Europe were simply destroyed by various methods. Some were ripped apart by tractors, blown to bits by grenades, raised and then dropped from cranes onto concrete blocks where they were smashed. There, and in the Pacific, steel cables were also used to pull the unwanted planes apart. In the Pacific war theatre, enormous junkyards on New Guinea, Biak, Guam, and in the Philippines contained hundreds of such machines, while still airworthy examples there were returned to the U.S. on escort aircraft carriers.

Among the more desirable of the surplus warplanes were transport types—C-47s, C-46s and C-54s. Many of these were sold or leased to form the foundations of post-war non-scheduled airlines and air cargo operations. Still another destiny for some of the war-weary planes was what was known as "the disposal of Surplus Aeronautical Property to Educational Institutions for Nonflight Use," in which aircraft were given to schools for the training of aircraft mechanics, and to cities and other communities to be used as war memorials. However, the level of support for the programme by many communities failed to match its scale in the minds of the government planners. It may be that educational value, historical significance, commemorative instincts, and any sort of nostalgia or sentimentality were simply outweighed by an overwhelming desire to forget everything about the war years and get on with the future. Thirty or forty years later that would change.

As a great number of veterans completed the bulk of their careers, raised their families, and achieved some of their ambitions, many paused to reflect on their own wartime experiences, which now seemed to have been an adventure rather than merely discomfort and misery. Some of them became interested in revisiting their old bases in England, Europe, Africa or the Pacific, places that held vague yet intriguing memories for them. Many did go back to see what was left of the sites where they had served. That compulsion was a part of what drove the warbird movement, a strange need to reach back across time and reconnect in some way with what, for many of them, had been the one great adventure of their lives.

By the summer of 1947, 65,000 ex-warplanes had been disposed of through the War Assets Administration. Of these, 35,000 had been sold for civilian use, while 10,000 were sold for scrap. The sales were slowing and only three of the major storage sites remained active.

The impact of the 1968 United Artists film *Battle of Britain* on the burgeoning warbird movement was major. In its background, the world-wide search by former RAF Group Captain and Stirling bomber pilot Hamish Mahaddie, for a stable of suitable Spitfires, Hurricanes, Messerschmitts and Heinkels provided the impetus for many enthusiasts and collectors to pursue their own warbird dreams. He located and arranged the loan of nineteen Spitfires and three Hurricanes, as well as for the maintenance facilities at RAF Henlow in Bedfordshire and the assistance of twenty-one RAF fitters. With the help of former Luftwaffe General Adolf Galland and RAF Group Captain R.L.S. Coulson, British Air Attaché in

Madrid, Mahaddie got the use of seven Hispano HA 1112 Buchons and more than fifty Casa 2.111s (Spanish versions of the Messerschmitt Me-109 and Heinkel He-111, respectively) in the filming. He also provided two Casa 352s (Spanish-built Junkers Ju-52 transports). The movie, the publicity surrounding it, and the peripheral involvement of the Battle of Britain veterans Galland, Al Deere, James 'Ginger' Lacey, Douglas Bader, Peter Townsend, Johnny Kent, Robert Stanford Tuck, Tom Gleave, and Lord Hugh Dowding, sparked substantial interest in the growing warbird community. It considerably advanced the cause of preserving the historic aircraft, as did the subsequent television series *Piece of Cake*, based on the Derek Robinson novel about a squadron of RAF fighter pilots in France in 1939 and 1940.

FLYING MUSTANG

"There were one-cushion pilots and two-cushion pilots, and if you didn't use a dinghy buckled to the D-rings of your back parachute, there were three-cushion pilots. Early in 1944, the Air Corps decided that a man five feet eight inches or shorter was a hot fighter pilot. If he was taller, he was destined for multi-engined flying. Thus, if a fighter pilot was fortunate enough to be selected to fly the P-51 Mustang, the multiplicity of cushions was necessary to boost him high enough to see out of the massive bubble canopy."

John A. De Vries was a member of the 40th Fighter Squadron, 35th Fighter Group in 1946, at Johnson Army Air Base in Japan the year after the Second World War ended. "The monsoon rains had come early that year and the base was socked in for the last half of September. I had plenty of time to study the lean and wiry Mustang before I flew it the first time. The squadron owned twenty-five of the bubble-canopied beauties, but only fourteen pilots were assigned, and there were plenty of 'ponies' to choose from. My choice was number 56—a K model. The P-51K differed from the D only in the particular that it had an Aero Products propeller instead of a Hamilton Standard.

"While the relentless rains fell, I studied the one and only P-51 flight manual available in the squadron. Not the usual 'Dash One,' the manual was a how-to-fly-it book, filled with cartoons and simple illustrations that emphasized the important factors for achieving maximum performance from the Mustang. Because the first flight would be solo, every word was important!

"The rains continued well into October, providing opportunity for three activities prior to checkout. And many, many hours were spent just sitting in the snug cockpit of No. 56

while the monsoon beat against the hangar roof. Gear handle, flap handle, throttle, mixture control, and propeller knob all fell closely at hand. The instrument panel was memorized as well as the armament control panel (which held switches for the six .50 caliber Brownings, the gunsight aiming point 16mm camera, the arming controls for the twin bomb or long-range tank wing pylons, and the rheostat that adjusted the intensity of the light in the reflector gunsight). The 'triggers' for all of the armament were clustered on the control stick hand grip. Soon I was able to pass the required 'blindfold cockpit check'—touch any instrument or control instantly, without any visual reference.

"The squadron was only at half-strength as far as pilots were concerned. The crew-chief situation was even more desperate. There weren't any. Two Master Sergeants made up the entire mainenance section. They, together with the North American Technical Representative for the Group, established a crew-chief school for pilots. For eight weeks, we new Mustang drivers attended classes every morning and worked on our own planes every afternoon. Changing the twenty-four spark plugs of the 1,400 hp, twelve-cylinder V-1650-7 Packard Merlin engine is a darn good way of finding out what goes on inside the Mustang. When I was ready to make my first P-51 flight, I really knew its innards.

"The weather began to clear enough for flying in the pattern. But before we new pilots were turned loose in our superbly maintained fighters (after all, we were our own maintenance crews), we had to go through the ordeal of rear-seat landings in the AT-6. The idea was that if you could land the skittery trainer from the back seat, you would do well 'when it came time' in the Mustang. However, the 'powers that be' failed to realize two important facts: the almost 1,000 hp difference in the engines of the two planes and that unless one were a giant, the overturn structure of the AT-6 effectively blanked out any forward vision.

"With six controlled crashes in the AT-6, I was really ready for my first Mustang ride. The walk-around inspection wasn't really necessary. I knew every rivet and Dzus fastener on No. 56. To please the check pilot, I approached my mount from the left. No bird's nests in the left wheel well; the sole landing light was firmly bolted inside. No oil dripping from the underside of the Merlin, and all of the cowl sections were firmly attached.

"The big, four-bladed Aero Products propeller was nick-free, and the carburetor intake under the nose was clear. No drips or loose Dzus fasteners on the right side of the nose, and the right tire (like the left) was brand new and properly inflated. The oleo strut spaced out to the proper hand-span, and the leading edge of the right wing was smooth. Aileron and the dropped flap looked 'right,' and the fuselage-mounted alternate static air source was clear of any foreign substances. The tail assembly looked OK—the fabric-covered movable surfaces were taut (later, the elevators would be replaced with metal-sheathed surfaces). A quick glance at the left aileron and flap, and then it was time!

"The hangar hours had proven to me that I was a two-cushion pilot. Two cushions and a dinghy (the CO2 cylinder which my gluteus maximus would soon learn to hate) propped me to the proper eye level—the center of my vision coincided with the pipper in the center of the gunsight (the P-51Ds in the squadron had gyro-stabilized K-14 sights.) With a casual familiarity born of many hours of cockpit time, I buckled myself in and began the round-the-cockpit check: ignition off, mixture-in-idle cutoff. "Capt. Bill Hook, the check pilot, pulled the prop through four blades to clear oil from the cylinders. The fuselage fuel tank (over the left shoulder) was filled to eighty-five gallons (each gallon was good for one minute's flight). Flap handle up, carburetor air in the 'ram' position, trim set—5° of right rudder, ailerons at 0, and elevator at 2° nose down. The gear handle was checked down, and the propeller control was to be 'full forward' (full increase rpms).

"The throttle was opened to the 'start' position (about three-quarters of an inch forward). The altimeter was set to field elevation, and gyro instruments were uncaged. Control locks were released (a pin was pulled from the bracket that held the stick and rudder pedals, the bracket springing flat against the cockpit floorboards) and the rudder pedals adjusted (full back for us shorter pilots). With parking brakes set, both wing fuel tank levels were checked through their indicators in the floor (ninety-two gallons each), the supercharger switch was put in 'auto,' and the fuel selector handle was set to 'fuselage' and I was ready to start.

"With booster pumps on (to provide fuel pressure), magneto switch to 'both,' and battery and generator switches on, I had to pause for a moment and run the coolant doors open. Liquid-cooled, the Mustang had to have its radiator uncovered for starting. Although the doors in the rear belly of the P-51 were thermostatically controlled and operated automatically depending on the temperature of the 30% glycol— 70% water coolant mixture, their functioning had to be checked manually on the ground before starting.

"A couple of tweaks of the primer switch and I raised the cover of the starter switch. Held in the 'start' position, the lean Mustang shuddered violently as the big prop turned over. After a few rumbles, the Merlin caught. I advanced the mixture to 'run' and the oil pressure rose to the proper 50 psi almost at once. The manual said to idle the engine at 1,200-1,300 rpm. All gauges 'in the green' or coming up, the suction at 4.75 psi, and I was ready to taxi. Captain Hook, who had been kibitzing over my left shoulder during the starting sequence, then gave me a pat on the back and leaped to the ground. Thumbs-up—and he pulled the wheel chocks.

"Suddenly, I was alone in a rip-snorting bucking bronco. Easing the Mustang's throttle open slightly, stick forward to unlock the tail wheel, I was on my own. Out of the parking area, I eased the stick back to lock the tail wheel in its 12° taxi arc (6° right and left). Lordy, that nose was l-o-n-g! Unless I S'd the bird, I couldn't see anything in front of me. The positive action of the disc brakes helped me taxi.

"By the time I reached the run-up pad at the end of the runway, Hook had climbed the control tower and it was he who 'talked' me through the engine checks. Rpm to 2,300, check each magneto for not more than a 100 rpm drop (but no longer than fifteen seconds operation on a single magneto). Advance the throttle to thirty inches of mercury for one minute and exercise the propeller pitch-changing mechanism. A rapid glance around the cockpit—prop forward, supercharger auto, coolant auto, fuel booster on, hydraulic and suction pressures, oil pressure and temperature in the green, and I was ready to take the runway. Hook checked the pattern from his tower vantage point and gave the go-ahead.

"Gently, ever so gently, I advanced the big spade-grip throttle ('liberated' from a K-14-equipped D-model Mustang— a sexy touch in my N-9-equipped K). The Merlin wound up. At thirty inches, the bird was as docile as an AT-6; at forty inches it was like riding a tornado; at the full sixty-one inches of takeoff manifold pressure I was caught up in a hurricane! The tail came up voluntarily as I pumped rudders to keep up with the enormous torque of the mighty engine. I could see over the nose, and the far end of the runway was approaching at an alarming rate.

"Somewhere along the route I'd attained flying speed, so a tug on the stick and No. 56 was blasting heavenward. Behind my left hip was the gear handle and I clutched it before I exceeded the 225 mph gear-door critical speed. The

Mustang did an involuntary dip as I raised the handle. Before I knew it I had reached 500 feet where the manual said I should throttle back to forty-six inches and pull the propeller control to 2,700 rpm for the climb.

"For the next hour and a half, I attempted to get ahead of my mount. The Mustang was a thinking pilot's airplane: think about it, and the airplane did it. There was enough pressure in thought alone to make 30° banked turns; rolls took only a wee bit of fingertip pressure. There was no combination of throttle, propeller, and trim tabs that would permit the Mustang to fly straight and level by itself. Oh, maybe its altitude would hold for five seconds before a bump would disturb its equilibrium, but hands-off, and the fighter would establish a climbing or diving spiral. You had to fly the P-51 every second you sat in the cockpit.

"A series of stalls—power on and power off, flaps and gear up and down—were part of the first ride. At 10,000 feet the book said, throttle back, dump gear and flaps, and slow the P-51 down to 125 mph. Simulate a final landing approach, and at the 'landing point,' jam on full throttle. It made me a believer: with a full sixty-one inches, old No. 56 turned every way but loose! I think I definitely did an inverted snap roll. I know the sturdy wings flapped. The point of the self-demonstration was to convince the neophyte pilot that the go-handle on the left side of the cockpit was to be moved deliberately but, oh so gently, particularly when the bird was near the ground.

"Landing time was fast approaching, so I headed east toward Johnson. I dove down into the Tokyo Plain at an easy-to-obtain 450 mph. With all of that Plexiglas around my head, the visibility from the cockpit was superb. No worry about running into another airplane.

"I saw a field and let down to 400 feet—tactical traffic pattern altitude. The hot Mustang was difficult to slow, but by pulling back on the big spade-grip throttle we got down to 240 mph indicated as required for pattern entry. Turning north, I stabilized speed and altitude and lined up with the strip. As the end of the runway passed under the Mustang's nose I pushed the propeller control to 2,700 rpm and honked the throttle back to idle. A sharp rightward and rearward tug on the stick, a boot of right rudder, and I was in a hairy chandelle. At its apex, I dumped gear and flaps (at about 180 mph) and continued around my 360-overhead pattern. Depressing the throttle-mounted microphone button, I called, 'Base leg!'

" 'Don't see you,' said Captain Hook, calmly.

"I continued in my fighter pilot's pattern. 'Turning final,' I announced into the VHF radio.

" 'Still don't see ya', Hook replied.

"It was then that I looked up. I was perfectly lined-up and at the proper approach speed of 120 mph. But I was landing at Yokota—three miles south of Johnson. Coolly, I yanked the gear and flaps up and slowly fed the 100-octane to the Merlin.

"De Vries, where the hell are you?' Captain Hook blasted into the airwaves.

"'I'm on one heck of a long final,' I replied, trying to inject a note of confidence into my oxygen-mask microphone.

"The abortive approach to Yokota had been good practice. The traffic pattern and landing at Johnson were good—for a beginner. I didn't notice, until I'd parked No. 56, the big prop grinding to a halt, that my flying suit was drenched and that there was a pool of sweat in my oxygen mask. The Mustang was a hot airplane in more ways than one! With only a couple of thin sheets of Dural between you and the Merlin, there was little protection from the engine's heat. But the heat was a small price to pay for the spectacular performance of the P-51—and it was very welcome on the missions above

20,000 feet.

"The engine stopped; I dumped the flaps to relieve the pressure on the hydraulic system and proceeded, round-the-cockpit, to turn every switch off.

"After twenty hours in No. 56, with the basics mastered, flying the P-51 became sheer joy. The 40th was a tactical fighter squadron so we were called on to perform every conceivable fighter mission. Today, it may be firing the six 50s at a towed sleeve over the Mito gunnery range or dive-bombing and strafing ground targets.

"When the machine guns let loose, the Mustang shuddered and bucked like its namesake and the flying speed dropped ten miles an hour. With the 100-mil fixed gunsight, I qualified for aerial gunnery—put forty bullets out of 200 into a banner target. Dive-bombing was easy: each diverging slash mark painted on the upper surface of the wings was associated with a specific bombing run entry altitude. As the target disappeared under the appropriate slash mark, you'd begin a diving turn onto the bomb run. The 'crack' on top of the forward fuselage, where the two removable cowling panels met, was the 'sighting line.' Point the crack at the target, roll to keep it lined up and kill the effect of the wind, and, at the proper release altitude, push the bomb-release button atop the stick. The 100-pound practice bombs would 'pickle' right on the bulls-eye!

"I love the hairy Mustang. With a single exception, every pilot I know who flew the P-51 loved it. The one 'sourpuss' was a B-24 driver who experienced two dead-stick landings and one bailout in his first three Mustang rides. But, this one individual notwithstanding, the pilots of the 15,000-odd P-51s that rolled from the North American production lines at Inglewood and Tulsa thoroughly enjoyed the calm—and the panic—of their hours in the $50,000 'Pony' "

Colonel De Vries retired from the U.S. Air Force with near

ly 5,000 flying hours in more than 100 types of military aircraft. He accumulated 800 flying hours in the Mustang.

WAR STORIES

"As the pilot of a B-26 Marauder bomber, I never saw a good dogfight. When enemy fighters got through our fighter cover they flashed past the formation so fast we saw only fleeting glimpses of them—and even that was too much. Our tail gunners saw a few skirmishes but no sustained engagements. When I finally did see one, it was from the ground.

"While flying my thirty-fifth mission, with the 344th Bomb Group to attack bridges across the Seine River near Paris on 28 May 1944, I was shot down by German flak. The following day I contacted members of the Resistance. They took good care of me and for five days I was hidden in a small tavern where I ate well and was treated royally as the guest of a fine couple, Carlos and Maria. They spoke excellent English, having spent many years in New York City where Carlos had led a rhumba band at the Waldorf-Astoria, and were glad to aid an American.

"On Thursday, 2nd June, I was moved to an apartment on the top floor of a building on the ruede Chantier in Versailles. There I was the guest of Charles and Delise. From their windows I could see the Eiffel Tower in the distance to the northeast. Less than four miles to the east I could see German aircraft taking off from Villacoublay aerodrome. At first there was only moderate activity, but on D-Day things really picked up, reaching a peak which was sustained for several days.

"Flights began arriving at dawn to refuel and fly shuttle runs to the invasion beachhead throughout the day. Often they returned individually, badly battered and damaged. Just before dark, they would refuel and fly to the more remote fields of eastern France to escape the night-bombing RAF. I was always amazed to witness their mass departures because they were so unorthodox compared with American techniques. "Their take-off procedure seemed to consist solely of a left climbing turn at maximum climb after gear-up. There was no regular interval between take-offs. Each plane departed when it was ready, started the left climbing turn and merged with the swirl of snarling aircraft.

"The first big mission departure I saw was on D-Day, before I learned of the Normandy landing a hundred miles or so to the west. It was about seven o'clock in the morning, and when I heard the sound of so many engines I pulled a chair over to the window and waited for something to happen. The revving of the engines continued, then suddenly a red-nosed Me 109 with red wingtips leapt up in a very steep angle, starting a left climbing turn. Others followed immediately, and with each new launch the stack grew higher and higher, forming one great, ever enlarging corkscrew-shaped spiral. When the last plane was airborne there must have been at least fifty fighters involved, and the whole shebang just seemed to collapse as the leader nosed his plane down, accelerating as the others tagged along in a sort of indiscriminate mass, behind, alongside, underneath and above him. Without an apparent pattern, they looked like a swarm of bees—either there was no precision or the utmost precision possible.

"I couldn't tell which was the case, but they never flew it any other way. I watched them many times and never saw them have any trouble, but I couldn't figure out how they could keep everyone in sight.

"That morning they headed westwards, and I wondered why such a large flight was in the area. It was far and away the largest I had seen, for most of the previous flights had been only small patrols.

"About two hours later, I heard several aircraft coming in from the west and looked out the living room window. The red-nosed Messerschmitt slanted hurriedly in, knifing down for a landing. There was a sense of urgency about it because he made no attempt to set up a preliminary pattern but maintained airspeed all the way through a long, straight-in approach. Before he touched down, out of sight behind the trees ringing the field, others flew in from the same direction. Several trailed smoke, one badly. Then another group came in, milling about over the field as they set up a landing priority. Some were Focke-Wulf Fw 190s. There must have been nearly a hundred fighters althogether. I remember counting more than sixty, and I missed several flights.

"Throughout the next half hour they continued to straggle in, revving their engines, jazzing them like kids in hot rods. The jazzing bit made me cringe. In B-26s we wanted power all the way in.

"A neighbour on a nearby balcony excitedly called Delise over and told her about the invasion. Delise came running inside, calling me by the name on my forged identity card which had said that I was a forty-two-year-old merchant from Deurdan.

" 'Albert, Albert, Le debarquement. Le debarquement est ici.' She was so excited I couldn't get much information from her. We turned on the radio, but German-controlled French station had nothing so I switched to the Yankee Doodle network. They were playing music—Glenn Miller. After a pause abd the phrase of the sone which identified the station, the announcer gave the latest report on the invasion, with a detailed analysis of the whole story. Then I knew where the Jerries had been and why their numbers had increased after take-off. The Luftwaffe was probably being diverted from all over Europe to Normandy. It was tremendous news, and to me it was a real boost. I kept listening to the radio all day and telling Delise what was happening. The French radio stations told us nothing, but all morning cryptic messages were

happening. The French radio stations told us nothing, but all morning cryptic messages were transmitted over both AFRS and the BBC. The BBC's were delightful.

" 'Pierre, there is a red, red rose in the icebox for you.'

" 'Marcel, your interest will be due on the 12th.'

"I often tuned to the BBC after that to catch those messages and to get the news at dictation speed, which gave me a chance to take notes.

"Later, one of our own teams went into action. Charles learned that the marshalling yard was full of German tanks which were supposed to depart for Normandy that night. I wrote a note to an English agent who had contacted me, and he got the message off by portable radio units at about eight o'clock in the evening. Just before midnight it got results, for the RAF started a raid which lasted until one a.m. The marshalling yard was closer to our apartment than I had thought, and for the entire raid there were flashes from exploding bombs, crumbling buildings, the thudding wham of anti-aircraft batteries and the almost constant rocking of our building on its foundation. We finally went to bed about three a.m.

"The next morning I was still sleepy and stayed in bed, dozing until something awakened me. It as an unfamiliar sound, a sort of popping. Then came sounds I recognized—racing aircraft engines. I jumped out of bed and ran over to the window, dragging the sheet with me. Coming straight toward me at not more than fifty feet above the roof was an American P-51 Mustang, going flat out. Close behind it were five Fw 190s, sort of bunched together, flying like the bees again, and all of them were taking pot shots with their 20mm cannon at the poor old Yankee boy.

"I saw all this simultaneously, before the planes flashed by just over the rooftop. They were coming from the airfield towards the apartment, headed north-west. I could even see the pilot, tensely hunched over the controls. He was wearing a helmet and goggles and his chute straps showed plainly against the darker color of his A2 jacket; a patch of white scarf was visible at his throat. The checquered yellow, or maybe checquered yellow and white, nose of his plane was clear and distinct. The aircraft was unpainted, bright aluminum, and its marking—black letters and the national insignia—stood out. It had a bubble canopy, the first one I'd ever seen.

"As they passed overhead, I whirled and ran through the apartment, across the living room to the window at the balcony on the other side of the building. The fighters actually dipped lower going away, for our building stood on the side of a slope, and the terrain fell away toward the center of Versailles. They were soon out of sight, and I was sure the P-51 jockey was a goner. I turned away from the window and for the first time realized Delise was standing by my side and that I was wearing only a pair of shorts.

"She looked at me and said, 'Albert, l'Américain?

" 'I think so, Delise, yes.'

" 'Ah . . . pas bon,'

"I went back into the bedroom and put on my pants and uppers. Then suddenly, Delise opened the door, shouting,

" 'Albert, ici, ici!'

"I followed her quickly into the living room and on to the tiny balcony. A couple of minutes had passed, with the battle unexpectedly continuing, but the tide had changed. Coming toward us from the south-west, still at roof-top level, were the six fighters, but leading the pack was a lonesome Fw 190, frantically trying to escape the P-51 pilot who was relentlessly hosing him with .50 caliber slugs in short, accurate bursts. Behind were the other four Jerries, holding their fire for fear of hitting the first Fw 190. Not more than 300 yards separated the first plane from the last.

"I began to really sweat out the American, though, because the Jerry was playing it cosy by heading straight for an anti-aircraft battery in a patch of woods. Sure enough, it opened fire. The Fw waggled his wing and the ground fire stopped, but the P-51 did the same thing and they didn't shoot at him either. Its pilot continued firing, and the law of averages caught up with the German plane. It exploded in a great, angry, red and black and orange burst.

"The Mustang pilot flew through the debris, but he was again the hunted and being shot at, so he banked toward Villacoublay a mile or so away. As he started a low pass over the field, all the ack-ack in the base opened up, even on their own planes. The three on the left, nearest Paris, turned left to avoid the flak, but the other one was too far to the right and had to turn to the right to stay clear. The Mustang turned also, heading for the lone Fw which apparently lost sight of him momentarily. Within thirty seconds the Yank was sitting on his tail, taking pot shots at the Luftwaffe again. The two planes were now heading toward me, almost on the same track they had flown on their first pass over the house earlier. The other three were completing a wider turn and were grouped some distance behind, and even though no physical change had occurred, they didn't seem to have the pouncing snarl or the look of the hunter so apparent in their first low-level pass. They straggled, trying to catch up, but they were too far back to save their buddy.

"Again I raced through the apartment to the other window. As the two planes came over, the thunder of their engines was punctuated by the short, ammo-saving bursts of the .50 calibers. Then, scraping over the rooftops, twisting and yawing, they crossed the city, and finally the Fw began to trail smoke. It nosed down into the horizon to merge with the red flame and black smoke-cloud of impact just west of town. (We learned later that the pilot got out alive but was badly injured.)

"The Yank racked the 51 around in a steep chandelle, right off the deck, almost reversing course. Two of the other 190s flashed past and pulled up also, but the third was a little further back and turned north, away from the tiger who continued his turn, diving a little now. With the height advantage for the first time, the Yank began firing on a dead pigeon. Smoke immediately trailed from the Fw, but the 51 pilot had to turn away as the other two planes closed in on him. The distressed Fw 190 limped away, trying to get back to Villacoublay, but crashed north of town several miles from the base. Now only two Germans were left, and the American had put a little distance between their planes and his.

"By this time I was absolutely going nuts. It was all I could to keep from shouting in English. Everybody else was excited too. People had come out on the rooftops of nearby apartments, and the balconies were full of men and women silently cheering for the crazy, lone American. I knew he would have a rough time from here on out. The last two wouldn't give him any breaks. On the other hand, they were wary, which might be in his favor. They flew out of sight on the deck southwest of the city. It was quiet for a minute or two and the rooftop audience became restless, frustrated.

"They they returned, still on the deck, and the Yank was miraculously in the middle. They made a long pass across town while the Mustang closed to a range from which he couldn't miss—I figured he was very low on ammunition. The 190 was trying to outrun him this time, but when he saw his nemisis so close behind, the pilot pulled up frantically. The .50s cut loose in a brief, shattering blast. The 190 nosed straight up and its engine died. As the prop windmilled almost to a stop, the plane began to stall about 1,000 to 1,500 feet off the deck, and the pilot bailed out, opening his parachute immediately. At first its slow, billowing trail made me think it would never open, but it blossomed full and white only a few feet above the trees between me and the Eiffel Tower, standing very tiny in the distance.

"Now the odds were even-up, and what had seemed an eternity to me had really happened in just a few minutes. I began to worry about other German fighters getting airborne to aid their shot-up air patrol, but they were either engaged elsewhere or were unable to fuel up, fearing attack from other aircraft.

"In the distance I could see the last two planes in another long, low arc. The American had started a gradual swing to the west, but he was not about to leave the deck. The Jerry was still behind him, but his guns were silent now, indicating he might also be low on ammunition. When they disappeared over the rim of the rolling hills west of the city the Mustang was taking evasive action, and I was sure the dogfight was almost over. The Jerry had the advantage and was sure to hold it. A moment later, a black, blotchy mushroom of smoke billowed upwards.

"I knew then that one hell of a good pilot had bought the farm. He had given it everything he had and reduced the odds from five to one to even before the end, and I wondered what he had thought when only that one Fw remained. Just a few pilots had ever shot down five German aircraft in one day.

"I noted the time and tried to fix the approximate location of the action and also made a mental note of the aircraft markings, determined to confirm the four victories if I ever got back to England. I just couldn't forget the way the man had flown, dreaming up tactics as he went along, playing it by ear, only to have his luck run out a little too soon.

"The spectators on the rooftops felt as I did. They stood up slowly, gestured with their hands and went back inside. They seemed to feel a personal loss, almost as if they had been with the pilot themselves, pushing him on to victory with their will alone. They had prayed for his survival, now they prayed for his soul.

"Delise said nothing but went into the kitchen and returned with two glasses and a bottle of Armagnac. She filled the glasses, raised hers and said, 'Le pilote Américain.' Her voice was soft and her eyes brimmed.

"I nodded and we drank.

"I had a couple more—alone.

"I sat there thinking about the pilot and the action-packed few minutes just passed. Suddenly, after three weeks of almost no war at all, it was back with me again and then suddenly gone. All I could do was sit there and think.

"Twenty minutes later, Charles, Delise's husband, came home. He was very excited and laughed as he asked if we'd seen the fight.

" 'Did you see the American kill those Germans?'

" 'Yes,' I said, 'We saw. He got four of them. Four out of five.'

He looked at me and grinned, taking another sip of brandy, and suddenly I wanted to hit him, he looked so smug.

" 'Non. No, no! He got five. He got them all. I see . . . everything. Especially the last. It was magnificent.'

"He said this in a mixture of French and English, the way was always conversed. I wasn't sure I understood. He launched into a stream of French I couldn't understand, but it didn't make any difference because I could tell he was certain the Yank had gotten all five. We had several more brandies before Charles calmed down enough to explain what had happened.

" 'Charles, how do you know he got them all?'

" 'Because I saw. Especially the second, third, and fifth, you know? The last was near me. I was at the garden. I have to rake—to hoe, you see? The last one he did not even shoot—much. They came near, so fast. There is this little hill, with woods. The planes almost skim the ground. The American goes zip, like so, around the hill once, and the German follows, but in a greater circle. It is like the cat and mouse. Then the second time the American plane slows—abruptly—its wheels drop out, you know? The German goes in, towards the American, now so much slower, and they are almost sideways, but he loses control of his machine. Only a kilometre or so from where I was standing he crashes into the woods. I jump up and down and wave my hoe and everybody does the same, but then the Germans come and we hide our smiles and I come home fast.'

"I thought about what must have happened. The American pilot was out of ammunition and had dropped his flaps and gear—everything—chopped his throttle, to slow down, forcing the German to turn in, risking a stall to make the German stall. The German didn't have much choice. If he didn't make one last try he would have wound up in front of the Mustang anyway—so he had made the try.

"Everybody I saw for the next few days talked about the dogfight. And coming so soon after D-Day, it gave all of us, me especially, a tremendous boost in morale.

"The plans to get me out of France by a night pick-up from a wheatfield didn't materialize, and it was early September before I reached London. I reported the dogfight during my debriefing, but by that time I had forgotten a key factor—the aircraft marking, including the squadron code.

"Many years later, I spent several days in the Air Force Historical section at Maxwell Field, Alabama, trying to learn the name of the pilot by reading all operational reports submitted by Mustang pilots for the period. (Now I do not even remember the exact date.) I narrowed it down to twenty-one pilots. Several were killed on the missions involved and others had been killed later in Germany. One noted 'confused fighting at house-top level in the Paris area' but claimed no victories.

"As of now, the identity of the American pilot has never been verified, and it's too bad. But there's one thing I know. Even if I never find out who he was—it was the best damned dogfight I'll ever see!"

—1st Lieutenant Henry C. Woodrum, formerly with the 344th Bomb Group (M), 9th USAAF

The black pilots of the 332nd Fighter Group, Eighth USAAF in the Second World War had shared a common experience with their white counterparts of the 4th Fighter Group. Both groups had been relatively rapidly transitioned from the plane they had been flying, to the new, very promising, very challenging P-51 Mustang. With the men of the 4th, it had been a matter of "You can learn to fly 'em on the way to the target", as their group commander, Colonel Don Blakeslee had told his boys the day they had flown their Thunderbolts over from Debden to the Steeple Morden base and traded them for the hot new fighter from North American Aviation. Blakeslee, when pleading with VIII Fighter Command chief General Bill Kepner to re-equip the 4th with Mustangs, had said, "Most of my boys flew liquid-cooled types in the RAF. It won't take them long [to transition.] As for the mechanics, don't forget they worked on Spitfires when the group first started to operate. Don't worry about them. General, give me those Mustangs and I give you my word—I'll have 'em in combat in twenty-four hours." Normally, pilots were given at least 200 hours of flying time in the Mustang before being sent into combat in the plane. The pilots of the 4th had been given on average just forty minutes each in the Mustang before flying their first combat mission in it. In his fine book *1,000 Destroyed*, former 4th Fighter Group public relations officer Grover Hall wrote: "Unfamiliarity with the plane and engine failures, chiefly overheating through coolant leaks, caused some pilots to be lost over enemy territory or to have narrow squeaks in emergency landings. But Don Blakeslee had willed it and the fact was he was right up there with them taking precisely the same risks. Otherwise, some probably would have refused to go. The P-51 was Seven League Boots: the Luftwaffe was presently to find that there was no such thing as recoiling beyond American fighter range anymore. The Mustang had a relatively low fuel consumption and the engineering resource had packed it with extraordinary capacity in the wings and fuselage. In addition, it carried not only one belly tank, but two wing tanks which were jettisonable. It was, moreover, a fighter which fought at both high and low altitudes. No other air force had anything comparable with the Mustang."

Still, the 4th FG paid a price for its move into Mustangs, suffering the loss of some of its finest and most promising young pilots in the change. So too, did the 332nd, the Red Tails, or Tuskegee Airmen as they were known. The pilots of the 99th Fighter Squadron of the 332nd FG, also paid a similar price in the summer of 1944 when they began flying their first Mustang missions, escorting bombers of the Fifteenth USAAF to Mediterranean targets. Mac Ross, who had been operations officer for the 99th, was killed on 10 July when the P-51B he was checking out fell into a descent and seemingly inexplicably went into the side of a hill. An apparent failure of his oxygen system was blamed for the crash. The following day brought the loss of Captain Leon Roberts whose P-51C plunged into the sea from high altitude, an event also attributed to possible hypoxia.

The world in the 1930s and 1940s faced the spreading threat of fascism as Japan and Nazi Germany went on the march to gain living space, resources, in fluence and domination. The self image of the American people in those days was one of free-spirited tolerance and equality, freedom and liberty for all. The contrast between that perception and reality, however, was stark. Certainly, for most black Americans, especially in the American south, reality was a very different thing. Racial segregation dominated life there as it always had. The rule was separate facilities and a separate way of life for all blacks. And among the most flagrant examples of this discriminatory attitude and behaviour was that of the American military and in particular the U.S. Army. Blacks in the army had long been, and continued to be, positioned in what were established as service units where they were wholly engaged in maintenance and basic labour activity. As for the navy, the only rate available to them then was that of mess attendant.

As organizational policy and attitudes trickle down from the top, and the views of many top officials of the American military establishment were, in racial matters, something less than enlightened, progress and tolerance for the black serviceman in the U.S. Army and Navy were all but non-existent. However, that began to shift very slightly in 1938 with the announcement by President Franklin D. Roosevelt of the formation of the Civilian Pilot Training Program in which more than 20,000 American college students were to be trained to fly every year. Students attending black schools were not included in the program initially. In the spring of the following year, though, an event occurred that changed the course of aspiring black airmen in the U.S. military. Two black fliers, Chauncey Spencer and Dale White, took off on a promotional flight from Chicago to Washington DC in their well-worn biplane to drum up interest in aviation for black Americans. Their arrival in the capital was noted by Harry S. Truman, a relatively unknown senator from Missouri who one day would become the U.S. president. Truman was intrigued by the fliers' effort and arrange to meet with them. He is reputed to have told them: "If you guys had guts enough to fly that thing from Chicago, I've got guts enough to do all I can to help you." Soon after that the U.S. congress appropriated funding to extend the Civilian Pilot Training Program, opening it up to students at black universities as well as to black students in white colleges. Through the course of the Second World War, 2,700 black pilots were trained in the CPTP program. A later addition to the program was the Tuskegee Institute, a black school near Montgomery, Alabama.

By early 1940, with the help and labour of students from Tuskegee Institute, a small airfield was constructed on a plot of land about forty miles from Montgomery. The program was up and running successfully at the airfield, leading to the beginning of a second course of aviation instruction for black pilots at another Alabama airfield, that of Alabama Polytechnic Institute in Auburn.

Success in the program at Tuskegee and soon donations by alumni led to construction of a larger, far more capable airfield facility on the Tuskegee site. With the participation of charitable organizations, including the Julius Rosenwald Fund, the progress of the program at Tuskegee was growing, and advanced more with the interest of one of the fund's board members, Mrs Eleanor Roosevelt, the wife of the president.

According to one account of the events of 29 March 1941, when the First Lady visited the airfield at Tuskegee, she allegedly asked the chief flight instructor "Can negroes really fly airplanes?" "Certainly we can; as a matter of fact, would you like to take an airplane ride?" he replied.

Much to the concern of her Secret Service protectors, Mrs Roosevelt requested and was taken on a flight by the chief flight instructor at Tuskegee, C. Alfred Anderson. Thereafter she remained a staunch supporter of black pilots in American aviation, a cause to which the Rosenwald Fund contributed generously. And Eleanor wasn't the only Roosevelt to come to the aid of the current and would-be black airmen. The president himself got involved in their cause in October 1940, prior to the presidential election. With an eye towards the support of black voters, and a shared interest with his wife in the development of aviation for black Americans in the period leading up to the virtually inevitable world war, he declared that "black Americans would serve in numbers proportionate to their representation in the U.S. population, in combat and non-combat roles alike."

In a truly bizarre example of military double-think, the U.S. Army Air Corps came up with a plan to develop an all-black air pursuit squadron together with the necessary units for its support. At the same time, the Air Corps continued its strict policy of rejecting the applications of black candidates for aviation training. The reason given by the service for the denial of these applications was invariably that there were no black units to which the men could be assigned. Eventually, a Howard University student, Yancey Williams, brought a law suit against the Army and forced it to admit him as a student pilot. The action caused the Army to implement its scheme for an all-black squadron, triggering the appropriation of $1 million for the construction of the ultimate Tuskegee Army Air Field. Additionally, the Army decided it was time to promote one of its better officers, Benjamin O. Davis, Snr., who happened to be black, to brigadier general, the first black American to be elevated to flag rank. Six months later, in July 1941, Davis' son, U.S. Army Captain Benjamin O. Davis, Jnr., together with eleven black cadets, was admitted to Class 42-C at Tuskegee for military aviation training. Davis, Jnr. was, at that time, one of only two black, non-chaplain officers in the entire U.S. Army.

Benjamin O. Davis, Jnr. had attended the United States Military Academy at West Point. There he had become used to the racial discrimination in vogue at the time, having been given the formal 'silent treatment' throughout his four year military education. Outside of official duties, no one spoke to him, and in all that time he was issued enough demerits for imaginary infractions for him to be dismissed from the Cadet Corps. However, the Commandant of Cadets interceded on Davis' behalf, voiding many of the demerits and enabling him to graduate.

In his final year at West Point, Davis had become interested in the possibility of army aviation and applied for flight training. His application was denied. Later, though, when the Army went ahead with its plans for development of an all-black squadron, Army officials realized that in Davis they had a perfect candidate to command the new unit.

That choice, however, did not alter the views of many at the top of the service who were determined that no black officer would ever command white men. And when Davis was given his initial flight physical examination at Fort Riley, Kansas: "The flight surgeon who gave me the exam did what all flight surgeons were doing when they had black applicants', he wrote down that I had epilepsy, and I was not qualified for flying training." Once again the Army double-think intervened and Davis was flown down to Maxwell Army Air Base, Alabama, where he underwent a second physical exam which countermanded the result of the first exam, and the captain was soon under training at Tuskegee.

The Army's selection of Captain Davis to command the 99th Fighter Squadron was a logical and appropriate one, but Davis was not a natural pilot. The Tuskegee director of flight instruction, Noel Parrish, was required to devote extra time with the officer to bring his flying skills up to an acceptable level. His other skills, though, including his leadership capability, left little to be desired.

The 99th Pursuit Squadron was activated on 19 March 1941 at Chanute Field, Rantoul, Illinois, with an initial cadre of

271 enlisted men training in aircraft ground support trades. It was to be the core of the black squadrons to be formed at Maxwell and Tuskegee airfields. Benjamin O. Davis, Jnr: "In organizing the 99th Pursuit Squadron, the Air Corps made a positive effort to avoid the worst aspects of segregation by creating an authentic and highly professional flying unit, similar in all respects to white pursuit squadrons except for the color of its personnel. In March 1941 the Army called for volunteers on a first-come, first-serve basis for the squadron, which was to be composed of 35 pilots and a ground crew of 278 men . . .

"Looking back, it seems clear to me that the Air Corps set and maintained high qualification requirements for the 99th. The corps made a conscious effort to select the best black aircraft maintenance, armament, communications, and supply people that the basic training centers could produce. Black enlisted people already in the service were undoubtedly selected because of their high qualifications and expressed desire. The cream of the crop of black enlisted personnel was available at the time, and from personal experience I can attest that the people assigned to the squadron were highly qualified. The requirement for two years of college was later eased as we approached Pearl Harbor and the Air Corps tried to find qualified applicants for pilot training who had not been to college.

"I was convinced that my professional future in the Air Corps would have to be based upon my own qualification as a pilot and assuming command of the 99th. On 19 July 1941, General Weaver addressed us at a ceremony at Tuskegee Institute inaugurating the flying training of blacks. 'The eyes of your country and the eyes of your people are upon you,' he said. 'The success of the venture depends upon you . . . You cannot be inoculated with the ability to fly . . . The life of a flying student is no bed of roses . . .' "

When flying training began for the new students at Tuskegee, the living conditions were something less than ideal. They were housed in tents and their mess hall had a dirt floor that became mud when it rained. The separately-quartered white personnel at the Tuskegee Field base dined in a mess hall withtablecloths and uniformed black waitresses served them. It was the American south in the 1940s, the American Army of the time, and segregation was still the way of life in that context.

The training experience at Tuskegee was not without racial incident. The initial base commander, Major James Ellison, believed strongly in the black airmen project, determined to do all he could to make it work. At one point, though, an event occurred in the town of Tuskegee requiring a black military policeman to take custody of a black enlisted man who was under arrest in the town jail. In the incident, the MP and his driver were also arrested, requiring the intervention of Major Ellison to arrange their release by the town authorities. The incident enraged the local residents, who were already angry about the presence of "armed negroes" on the nearby base. Soon Major Ellison was relieved of his command and quickly replaced by Colonel Frederick von Kimble, who dealt with the situation by segregating the base. He had signs posted labelling the facilities for 'white' or 'colored' use. Captain Davis reflected on von Kimble's period in command as "turning the base into a prison camp, with the students frightened of the prevailing racial climate on the base."

Von Kimble is alleged to have believed that the blacks at Tuskegee lacked leadership ability and that while he was in command there, no black would achieve a rank higher than captain. Following a War Department investigation into von Kimble's conduct, he too was relieved of command and was replaced by Colonel Noel Parrish, the base director of flight instruction. Parrish, unlike von Kimble, was totally devoted to achieving success in the training of the black pilots there at Tuskegee, working hard to moderate and resolve tensions between the town residents and the base personnel and making great strides to improve the situation. Sensitive to the difficulties faced daily by the men under his command, Parrish did what he could to minimize if not entirely eliminate the segregation on the base and to raise morale by arranging for entertainment visits by Louis Armstrong, Lena Horne, Ella Fitzgerald, Joe Louis, and others. He also did his best to contain the efforts of those in Washington who were determined to bring an end to the black pilot training program. Parrish instead petitioned Washington officials to allow his Tuskegee airmen to serve in combat.

Davis: "Parrish is the man who proved that blacks could fly an aeroplane. In those days, to whites, blacks couldn't do anything very well, except dance and sing. Blacks supposedly couldn'g fly aeroplanes because that was too technical, and Parrish proved they could. He held the future of blacks in the Army Air Corps in his own little hands. Anybody, everybody should be extremely grateful to Parrish for his performance of duty. He wasn't doing anybody any favors— he was performing his duty conscientiously in a way that benefited everybody, to include the United States Army Air Force."

Progress for the Tuskegee airmen continued, but at a slow pace. The persistent double-think policies allowed racial segregation went on despite a pressing need to modify them in the face of technical training demands. One example was the process of developing separate African-American flight surgeons to support the operations and flight training of the Tuskegee airmen. Prior to the development of this unit, there were no black flight surgeons in the U.S. Army. Black Army medical examiners had previously been trained via correspondence courses. Then, in 1943, two black physicians were finally admitted to the U.S. Army School of Aviation Medicine located at Randolph Field, Texas. From 1941 through 1949, a total of seventeen flight surgeons served with the Tuskegee airmen in a typical four-year tour of duty in Alabama, North Africa, Italy, and Sicily. Vance Marchbanks, Jr. was the chief flight surgeon to the Tuskegee airmen. He had been a childhood friend of Benjamin O. Davis, Jr.

The combat-ready 99th Fighter Squadron shipped out of Tuskegee on 2 April 1943, bound for North Africa. There it was to join the 33rd Fighter Group under the command of Colonel William Momyer. Their first actual combat mission was an attack on the strategic volcanic island of Pantellaria in the Mediterranean, a part of the Allied effort to clear the sea lanes for the invasion of Sicily in July, the air assault for which began on 30 May 1943. That initial mission of the 99th was flown on 2 June. At that early stage, the men of the 99th were assigned to a basic ground attack role, which while important, did prevent their engagement in aerial combat activity for the time being.

In late February, the pilots of the all-black 332nd Fighter Group had been ordered overseas with their three squadrons, the 100th, 301st and 302nd, all under command of the now Colonel Benjamin O. Davis, Jnr. The 332nd was then based on mainland Italy at Ramitelli Airfield, near Termoli on the Adriatic coast. There they were joined by the 99th Fighter Squadron. The bulk of their new role would be to escort the heavy bombers of the Fifteenth Air Force on their lengthy strategic bombing raids against enemy targets in Poland, Austria, Hungary, Germany, and Czechoslovakia. The pilots and the P-51 Mustang aircraft of the 332nd became known as the "Red Tails" for the bright crimson of their fighter's tail sections.

The 332nd Fighter Group and the 99 Fighter Squadron

were the only black air corps organizations to fly in combat during the Second World War. The 99th Pursuit Squadron had been re-named the 99th Fighter Squadron in May 1942 and during its wartime service it earned three Distinguished Unit Citations, for its air operations over Sicily, 30 May to 11 June 1943, Monastery Hill near Monte Cassino, 12 May to 14 May, 1944, and for its successful air action against Me 262 jet fighters on 24 March 1945. This last was the longest bomber escort mission of the Fifteenth Air Force of the war.

Colonel Benjamin O. Davis, Jnr: "[The] Army Air Forces had dodged the deployment decision for many months. Under the original plan, the 99th would have been sent to Roberts Field, Liberia, as part of a task force providing air defense to an important point on our line of communications to North Africa, the Middle East, and China. Apparently, AAF thought that it would be appropriate to assign its black fighter squadron to black Liberia to minimize racial troubles . . . But with the success of the Allied landings in North Africa in November 1942, the need for the air defense of Roberts Field was elim-inated . . . Finally, but also within the bounds of segregation, it was decided to move the 99th to North Africa in the spring of 1943 as a separate squadron in the Mediterranean theater.

"While no AAF unit had gone into combat better trained or better equipped than the 99th Fighter Squadron, we lacked actual combat experience. So as we approached our first mis-sions, my own inexperience and that of my flight commanders was a major source of concern. On the other hand, we had averaged about 250 hours per man in the P-40 (quite a lot for pilots who had not yet flown their first missions), and we pos-sessed an unusually strong sense of purpose and solidarity.

When the pilots of the 99th Fighter Squadron were upgrad-ed from the P-40 fighters they had long been flying, to the new, highly-rated P-51 Mustang, they liked the distinctive look of their new planes with their red tails and prop spinners. To the question of whether or not the bright red identity colour would actually make them easier targets for enemy aircraft, the response was a definite no. In fact, the majority of the new Mustang pilots believed that the red markings on their planes simply made their recognition easier for the friendly gunners in the bombers they were escorting.

The melding of the 99th into the 332nd group was not free of friction. By the time that occurred, the 99th had accrued considerable air combat experience, far more than the largely inexperienced men of the 332nd. The pilots of the 99th deeply resented the possibility that they would be ordered to fly as wingmen to the men of the 332nd. The pilots of the 332nd, on the other hand, tended to be resentful of the fame and achievements of the men of the 99th, and were concerned that assignment of the better missions scheduled would go to the 99th pilots. Fortunately, for all concerned, Colonel Davis was probably the ideal command personality to successfully join these slightly hostile forces and mold them into a really effective fighting unit.

One factor soon began to outweigh all others in the rapidly spreading reputation of the Tuskegee airmen. They quickly became known throughout the Fifteenth Air Force for the extremely high quality of the protection they provided when escorting the heavy bombers on their long, demanding raids. The safe escort they offered was revered by the grateful crews of the heavy and medium bombers they shepherded daily.

Forty-two Mustangs of the 100th, 301st, and 302nd Fighter Squadrons took off at 8:30 a.m. on 6 July 1944 from the air strip at Ramatelli; their mission that day to provide penetration, target cover and withdrawal cover for the bombers of the 47th Bomb Wing on their mission to Tagliamento, Latisana, and Casarsa. Of the forty-two fighters, four spares, one escort, and two mechanical failures returned early to Ramatelli. Two additional Mustangs made it as far as landfall on the Italian coast before having to turn back, and were given the mission credit. At just after 9:33 a.m., the remaining thirty-seven P-51s rendezvoused with the bomber force at various altitudes. The first two groups of bombers were covered by the fighters of the 100th at 22,000 feet. Responsibility for middle cover of the four bomb groups flying at 24,000 feet fell to the Mustangs of the 301st Squadron, with the fighters of the 302nd picking up the rear of the bomber formation at 29,000 feet. The raid went off largely without incident, though the formations were considered to have been too wide, making bomber wing recognition all but impossible. Lessons learned.

On 12 July the squadrons of the 332nd were briefed to fly an escort mission for the B-24 Liberators of the 49th Bomb Wing to a target in France. Their assignment was to provide close cover, escort penetration, target cover, and withdrawal cover for the bombers. The forty-two Mustangs lifted off from the Ramatelli base at 7:45 a.m. Six spare fighters and two suffering mechanical failures returned to base early. Rendezvous with the bombers took place at 10:11 a.m. in heavy overcast at 23,000 feet. By the time the bombers and their escorts reached the target area, the Mustangs of the 301st FS were in the lead, with those of the 100th in the middle, and the planes of the 302nd as the high squadron. Suddenly, as the force approached the target, approximately twenty-five German fighters were sighted near the French coast.

Several direct hits were noted by bomber crewmen as the big planes achieved a good bombing pattern on the target. At least twelve Fw 190 fighters were observed and more than thirty German ships were seen in the harbour at Toulon as the bomber and fighter force passed. As it neared the airdrome at Toulon, upwards of sixty enemy fighters were observed in the revetments around the airfield. Now, a half dozen Fw 190s were spotted peeling off from the ten o'clock position to the bombers. The German fighters slowly formed a line and dived down into and through the bomber formation, reaching a high speed of descent before entering a split "S" and going into a tight left turn followed by a second split "S". One of the 190s was hit by gunfire from one of the Mustang. Meanwhile, in the midst of the bomber force, a second Fw was hit and destroyed by the Mustang of Lieutenant Harold Sawyer of the 301st Fighter Squadron.

Another 301st Fighter Squadron pilot, flight leader Joseph Elsberry, caught sight of a flight of sixteen Fw-190s as they lined up to launch an attack on the bomber formation from the nine o'clock position. He ordered his pilots to drop their belly tanks and attack the 190s. On seeing the approaching P-51s, the German pilots chose not to fight, but Elsberry caught up with one of them and managed a quick deflection shot that found its mark on the left wing root of the Fw, which lost the wing immediately and began trailing thick black oily smoke from the the wound. The kill, though, went unobserved by the other American pilots, who were otherwise occupied with their own Focke-Wulfs. Elsberry would only be credited with a probable for the effort. Just then he saw another Fw slide into his sights and he opened fire, scoring hits in the left wing of the German plane which entered a roll followed by a split "S" as the American pilot continuted firing short bursts at him. In his effort to elude Elsberry, the German soon lost the battle and ploughed into the ground, becoming the first definite kill of the day for Joe.

Less than one minute passed before Elsberry was again in position to strike at another of the Focke-Wulfs that had got within firing range of the American. This time there could be no doubt about the fate of the enemy fighter. Two of Elsberry's associates witnessed his .50 caliber bursts finding vital bits of the Fw and sending it down to crash and burn. Mustang pilots Robert Friend and Charles Dunne saw and confirmed Joe Elsberry's second kill of the engagement.

Now as he watched, Elsberry noticed another Focke-Wulf passing in a forty-five degree descent to his right. Elsberry threw the Mustang into a hard right turn in an effort to keep the German in his sights. By this point, only his left wing guns were useable, but he got off a few brief, effective bursts that struck the enemy plane in the left wing. The German pilot tried to escape by putting his Fw into a tight spiral dive but was unable to pull out and went into the ground for Elsberry's third of the day. He became the first black American fighter pilot to be credited with three enemy aircraft downed in one day.

Despite a bright and impressive war record, controversy came along to dog the Tuskegee airmen many years after the end of the war. It actually began the prominent African-American weekly newspaper, the *Chicago Defender*, in its edition of 24 March 1945, while the Second World War still raged in both Europe and the Far East, published an article stating that no bomber escorted by the Tuskegee Airmen had ever been lost to enemy fire. The piece appeared under the headline: 332nd Flies its 200th Mission Without Loss. The information for the article had been supplied by the Fifteenth U.S. Army Air Force. For several years thereafter that statement about the record of the Tuskegee pilots was repeated, unchallenged, until various researchers took an interest in the claim and began looking into it.

Subsequent research has established that, of the 179 bomber escort missions flown by the 332nd Fighter Group in support of the bombers of the Fifteenth Air Force, only seven of those missions resulted in bomber losses for the Americans, for a total loss of twenty-five bombers, a figure far lower than that of the average number of bombers lost while under the escort of other Fifteenth Air Force fighter groups in that same period.

Colonel Benjamin O. Davis, Jnr: "On 2 July I led a twelve-plane escort of twelve B-25 [medium bombers] to Castelvetrano in wouthwest Sicily. It was on this mission that I saw my first enemy aircraft, an element of two Fw-190s and a flight of four Me-109s, far above my part of our formation, which was flying close escort to the B-25s. When the enemy planes dove on the bombers, our top cover turned into them and kept them out of range. During this mission we had our first pilot losses: Lts. Sherman White and James McCullin. We believed at the time that both these pilots had made forced landings along the Sicilian coast, but regrettably, it did not turn out that way. The loss of fighter pilots was like a loss in the family. On each combat mission, members of the squadron watched the take-off and were always on hand in large numbers to count the planes as they returned and greet the pilots. On the brighter side of that mission, Lieutenant Hall shot down an Fw-190, the first time a black pilot had downed an Axis plane, and damaged an Me-109. All our other pilots returned to base."

In January 2010, a ninety-year-old American fighter pilot, Lee A. Archer, Jnr., died in New Rochelle, New York. In the Second World War, Archer had been a pioneering member of the famous Tuskegee Airmen, the first black Ameican fighter pilots. Perhaps his greatest combat achievement took place on 12 October 1944 when he was involved in a furious series of dogfights over German-occupied Hungary. Within only a few minutes, Lieutenant Archer, flying one of his group's distinctive red-tailed P-51 Mustang fighters, engaged and shot down three German fighter planes. From his obituary in the *New York Times*, 3 February 2010: "At a time when the armed forces were segregated and the military brass was reluctant to give blacks combat responsibilities, the four squadrons of the Tuskegee unit proved time and time again that black pilots had the bravery and skills to escort American bombers to their targets and blow enemy planes out of the sky.

"Lee Andrew Archer, Jnr. was born in Yonkers on Sept. 6, 1919. He became enthralled with aviation as a youngster in Harlem Joining the Army out of New York University, hoping to become a pilot, he was assigned to a communications job at a post in Georgia because the Army did not want any black fliers. But when it began training black servicement to fly at its Tuskegee airfield in Alabama, Mr Archer joined the program and won his wings in the summer of 1943.

"When he returned home in 1945, a recipient of the Distinguished Flying Cross, he found that nothing seemed to have changed in American society.

" 'I flew 169 combat missions when most pilots were flying 50', Mr Archer told the *Chicago Tribune* in 2004. 'When I came back to the U.S. and down that gangplank, there was a sign at the bottom: 'Colored Troops to the Right, White Troops to the Left.'

"But he remained in the armed forces, which were desegregated by President Harry S. Truman in 1948, and retired as a lieutenant colonel in 1970.

"In October 2005, Mr Archer and two fellow Tuskegee veterans visited an air base at Balad, Iraq, to meet with 700 servicemen from a successor unit to his all-black outfit. 'This is the new Air Force,' he told The Associated Press. In the dining room, he said, he saw 'black, white, Asian, Pacific Islanders, people from different parts of Europe.' 'This,' he said, 'is what American is.' "

In their World War II combat history, the Tuskegee Airmen achieved the following: more than 15,000 combat sorties flown; 111 enemy aircraft destroyed in the air; 150 destroyed on the ground; 950 railcars, trucks and other motor vehicles destroyed; one destroyer sunk. Their losses included sixty-six pilots killed in action and accidents; thirty-two pilots downed and captured to become prisoners of war. Awards numbered 150 Distinguished Flying Crosses, 744 Air Medals, eight Purple Hearts, and four Bronze Stars.

Master Sergeant Merle C. Olmsted, died in January 2008. He was a member of the 357th Fighter Group of the Eighth Air Force, and a crew chief for the P-51 Mustangs flying out of Leiston Airfield, Suffolk, England in the Second World War. He very kindly permitted me to reprint portions of his article, *Last Seen in Combat Area*: "The 14th of January 1945 is a date that has received little attention from aviation historians, but it was, in fact, a major event in the history of aerial combat—one of the largest fighter vs. fighter air battles, in a war already heavily laden with such occasions, and one unlikely to be approached on such a scale again. For months, during that fall and winter, the Luftwaffe had been semi-dormant, occasionally reacting with vigor, and on other days, virtually ignoring the swards of allied warplanes. The magnet that drew them into battle this day was a force of B-17s bound for targets in the Berlin area, and although several Eighth Air Force fighter groups were involved in the battle, the 357th Group was first to engage and was to score the heaviest—their 'big day' as it is still called.

"On the evening of that day, as claims filtered in to 66th Fighter Wing (the 357th's parent unit), they generated considerable astonishment, and not a little skepticism. By the next day, however, the claim of 56 1/2 enemy aircraft destroyed was generally accepted as rechecks had failed to reduce the number, and it stands today as the largest number of victories scored by one group in Air Force history. Luftwaffe records tend to agree, and show very heavy losses, with JG 300 and JG301 (home defense units) reporting 78 aircraft lost in one battle that day.

"There was, however, another side of the story. Statistically, it had been overwhelmingly in the Yoxford Boys' favor, 56.5 victories for three pilots lost. Statistics, though, are of little comfort if you are one of those on the debit side, and it is these three, listed on the mission report as 'Last seen in combat area,' whose story we will tell here. Ultimately, all three of these men were among the fortunate—they survived their often hair-raising adventures, and two are still with us today, with the whereabouts of the third unknown. We will not attempt to relate the story of this vast air battle, except as background for one of our three 'Missing in Action' of the 357th Fighter Group, Lt George Behling, Jr.

"Fighter Station 373, which sprawled across the county of Suffolk, near the villages of Therbeton, Yoxford, and Leiston, had been occupied by the 357th Group and its supporting units since January of the previous year. Its nominal strength of 75 red-and-yellow-nose P-51s, about which all base activities centered, were scattered around the perimeter taxi strip on hardstands and revetments, some of which remain today, as the only reminder of station F-373.

"The 14th of January began as most other days had for the preceding year, with preparations in hand for mission No. 253, an escort to 3rd Division B-17s scheduled to bomb oil targets at Derben, in the Berlin area.

"Weather conditions at home station that morning were not ideal, with early morning fog giving way to low clouds, its base at about 1500 feet, with tops at between 3000 and 4000. Even so, it was one of the better days of the month of January, which saw a mean temperature of 33 degrees F., and runways either frozen or covered with snow 18 days. There was rain, drizzle or snow on 21 days of the month, providing very poor conditions for the maintenance or operation of fighters of that period.

"Despite the long period of poor weather, Eighth Air Force forecasters had been watching with considerable interest two high-pressure areas, one over the North Atlantic west of Ireland, the other over the northern part of Sweden and Finland, which provided hope of good weather over north-west Germany. The two eventually merged, forming a ridge of high pressure extending from the North Atlantic into Russia. By the 14th the ridge had begun to dissipate with cloud cover over Britain, with France and Belgium under patchy clouds. Over north-west Germany and the target area, however, there was only a trace of clouds with excellent visibility. It was this generally favorable weather which provided the backdrop for the great air battle of January the 14th, 1945.

"On the 17 days of the month when it had been possible to operate, takeoff time had been in midmorning, as it was on this day, the 66 Mustangs departing 1010 hours. There were, however, 10 aborts for various reasons, leaving Colonel Irwin Dregne with only 56 P-51s. Dregne, the Group Commander, was leading both the mission and the 364th Squadron (code name Greenhouse), which was to emerge from the day's action with claims of 21 1/2-0-2 and no pilot losses. Chester Maxwell, however, came home late and without his airplane.

"Major John England led the 362nd (Dollar) Squadron, reduced to 20 aircraft soon after landfall in which the seven-victory ace 'Dittie' Jenkins turned back with a rough engine, taking his wingman with him.

"Element leader in John Kirla's Dollar Green Flight was 1st Lt. George A. Behling, Jr., and his wingman, Green 4, was 2nd Lt. Jim Gasser. Green 2 on Kirla's wing was Lt. J.W. Dunn. George Behling was to be one of those 'Last seen in combat area.'

"Here is a portion of Colonel Dregne's mission report: 'R/V

1150 N. Cuxhaven 25,000 ft with 1st 3 combat groups of 1st force. L/F in 1201 N. Cuxhaven 26,000 ft. L/F out 1420 the Hague 20,000 ft. Group leader observed two gaggles of S/E E/A approaching bombers from southeast about 20 miles north of Brandenburg. Low gaggle at 28,000 ft consisting of 70-plus Fw 190s, with a top cover of 60-plus Me-109s at 32,000. Fw 190s were in company front approaching in waves of eight A/C. Our group intercepted, attacked, and in a 30-minute battle destroyed E/A listed above. [56 1/2-0-5 S/E air, 1-0-0 S/E ground, 2-0-0 locomotives. Author.] Combat was from 30,000 to deck. None of the formation of E/A attacked believed to have reached the bombers, although some may have filtered through. E/A were very aggressive when intercepted and fought it out. Engagement began at 1245 and continued until group had to leave for lack of fuel. Part of group reformed providing withdrawal support to bombers, leaving bombers 1350 north of Dummer Lake, 18,000 ft. During engagement another group of about 30 S/E E/A attacked bombers believed to be 5th or 6th C Grp. Several other P-51 groups seem to engage these E/A.'

"The day before Christmas saw the 357th flying two separate missions, both resulting in extensive combat with Luftwaffe fighters, and combined claims of 31 S/E E/A shot down. As they would on the 14th of January, Luftwaffe home defense unit JG300 suffered severely losing 18 pilots, one of whom was the leader of 5/JG300, a 31-victory ace Ritterkreuztrager Leutnant Klaus Bretschneider. During this melee west of the city of Fulda, George Behling shot down an Fw 190 and in light of this victory, his experience on 14 January was, he says, 'poetic justice.'

"The instrument clock on the escorting Mustangs was approaching 1240 hours as the force closed on the target area. Behling remembered: 'Berlin is easily discernible by the heavy black flak smoke at our altitude. Suddenly a maze of German pursuit planes came screaming down on us from above. The sky is filled with airplanes. I jettison my wing tanks and take a bead on an enemy fighter. A fellow P-51 drifts across my bow at a 30-degree angle in slow motion, so close I still don't know why I didn't tear off his tail with my propeller. I'm completely distracted and lose sight of my quarry.

" 'I bank to the left and look behind. There is a plane on my tail but it isn't my wingman. It has a large radial engine and is easily identifiable as an Fw 190. What happened to my wingman who was supposed to cover my tail in such a short period of time, to this day I have no idea.'

"Behling's wingman, Jim Gasser's mission report: 'When our squadron sighted a large gaggle of enemy fighters preparing to attack the bombers, we dropped tanks and started a diving turn to the left. In the pull-out I blacked out and when I recovered I found that my 'G' suit rubber hose connection had come loose. I also found myself alone. Lt. Behling was nowhere in sight. I called him over R/T and told him that he wasn't covered, but received no reply, for the radio was rather congested. In a few minutes I joined up with Lt. Kirla, who was leading our flight, and remained with him the remainder of the battle. I did not see nor hear Lt. Behling again.'

"Jim Gasser does not mention his encounter with an Fw 190 as it was not pertinent to Behling's loss, but his encounter report provides details of that action. When he recovered from his blackout, he spotted the skyblue 190 off to his left and immediately shot it down, the pilot bailing out. Gasser recalls: 'I was no doubt startled as to this dumb maneuver by the Kraut, but was awed at the beauty of his aircraft as well. There was no skill in his destruction.'

"With his wingman now gone due to a disconnected G suit, and an Fw 190 on his tail, we return to George Behling's own words to describe the traumatic events . . . that followed. 'Now I turn to the left. Left rudder, left stick, more throttle. I've got to outrun him. I see his cannon bursts but apparently he can't lead me enough. I wonder what I'm doing here; a person could get killed. Why did I ever want to be pilot? I'm only 20 years old and should be home, going to school and returning in the evening to my parents' comfortable home.'

" 'I pull into a tighter, tighter turn, feeling so many Gs I can hardly turn my head. Then the stick goes limp. I'm spinning—but you never, never spin a P-51 because it might not come out. My primary training instinctively takes over. I kick the right rudder hard. The plane stops spinning and I pop the stick forward. I'm flying again at 20,000 feet.'

" 'This time I turn to the right and look behind. The son of a bitch is still there. He followed me through a spin and 10,000 feet. It can't be. These German pilots are supposed to be undertrained, wet-behind-the-ears kids.'

" 'Same scenario. Tighter and tighter to the right. More cannon bursts. Another spin, coming out at 10,000 feet. He's still there.'

" 'Well, if I can't outturn him, surely I can outrun him. I shudder at the thought of one of those cannon shells tearing through my plane. In fact, I'm utterly paralyzed with fear. I point the plane at an approximated ten-degree angle toward the ground and open the throttle full. It's working, he's falling behind, out of range. Now I'm at treetop level west of Berlin passing over the Elbe River. My engine sputters, intermittently spewing white clouds. I cut back on the throttle and lean the mixture, but the sputtering gets worse. Suddenly the engine goes dead streaming two contrail-like bands from each side. Hurriedly, I try the starting procedure several times to no avail.'

" 'I'm directly over a dense forest. No place to land. Pull up and bail out. But I'm now going less than 200 mph. Not enough speed to pull up to an altitude that will give my chute time to open. Look for a place to put this baby down dead stick. Dead Stick! It was my worst thing in basic training. Without power I would have killed myself every time.'

" 'There—twenty degrees to the left is an open field running parallel to a railroad track. I'm barely flying so don't turn too sharply. The stick feels mushy. Easy, easy! I'm lined up, fifty feet above the ground, wheels up. Then, right in front of me high-tension wires. I close my eyes and pull back on the stick. Somehow (I don't know how, I wasn't looking, but perhaps the downwind landing helped!), I bounce over the wires and hit the ground with a thud. It's a frozen plowed field and my plane skids along like a sled. Up ahead is a line of heavy trees and I'm zooming towards them with no way to stop. But I do stop fifty feet short. Open the canopy. No one around. I hear the clickety-clank of an engine Look behind. There's the 190 coming right at me. Get out of this plane and get behind one of those trees. I get tangled in the straps so I crouch down behind the armorplate in back of my seat. The 190 doesn't strafe and passes overhead. Now, with him in full sight, I disentangle myself, get out of the plane and run for the trees. I make my way along the line of trees some 200 feet to the railroad embankment, go over it and head away. Up ahead is a bridge. But two figures on the bridge are coming toward me from the other direction. I stop and wait.'

" 'An officer approached me. He was a German colonel, home on leave from the Russian front, and spoke English. He said, 'For you the war is over. I bet when you took off this morning you didn't think you would be here this afternoon.' I replied with true survival instinct. 'Don't let those children in the cockpit; the guns are alive.' He shrugged and began marching me across a field toward a ditch. 'Okay, they'll just shoot me and lay me in the ditch.' How long could my luck hold out? But we went through the ditch and to a farmhouse where the colonel left me in charge of a farmer, his wife and their teenage daughter.' "

BIBLIOGRAPHY

Bekker, Cajus, *The Luftwaffe War Diaries*, Doubleday, 1968

Bishop, Edward, *The Battle of Britain*, George Allen & Unwin, 1980

Collier, Richard, *Eagle Day*, Pan Books, 1968

Deere, Alan, *Nine Lives*, Hodder & Stoughton, 1959

Deighton, *Len, Fighter*, Ballantine Books, 1977

Dwiggins, Don, *Hollywood Pilot*, Doubleday, 1967

Farmer, James, *Celluloid Wings*, Tab Books, 1984

Galland, Adolf, *The First and the Last*, Ballantine Books, 1954

Fry, Garry and Ethell, Jeffrey, *Escort to Berlin*, Arco, 1980

Gelb, Norman, *Scramble*, Michael Joseph, 1986

Godfrey, John, *The Look of Eagles*, Random House, 1958

Goodson, James, *Tumult in the Clouds*, St Martins Press, 1983

Hall, Grover C, Jr., *1000 Destroyed*, Putnam, 1946

Hall, Roger, *Clouds of Fear*, Coronet Books, 1975

Haugland, Vern, *The Eagle Squadron*, Ziff-Davis, 1979

Hess, William, *Fighting Mustang*, Doubleday, 1970

Hillary, Richard, *The Last Enemy*, Macmillan, 1950

Ilfrey, Jack, *Happy Jack's Go-Buggy*, Exposition Press, 1979

Johnson, Frank, *Roseanna's Reply*, Central Coast Press, 2008

Johnson, J.E., *Wing Leader*, Ballantine Books, 1957

Olmsted, Merle, *The 357th Over Europe*, Phalanx, 1994

Peaslee, Budd, *Heritage of Valor*, J.B. Lippincott, 1964

Toliver, Raymond & Constable, Trevor, *Fighter Aces*, Macmillan, 1965

Wagner, Ray, *Mustang Designer*, Orion Books, 1990

Willis, John, *Churchill's Few*, Michael Joseph, 1985

Wood, Derek & Dempster, Derek, *The Narrow Margin*, McGraw-Hill, 1961

Yeager, Chuch and Janos, Leo, *Yeager*, Bantam Books, 1985

Zemke, Hub and Freeman, Roger, *Zemke's Wolf Pack*, Orion Books, 1988

Aeroplane & Armamernt Experimental Establishment, 22
Air Fighting Development Unit, 22, 27
Allen, Edmund, 84, 85
Allison V-1710, 19, 21, 29, 33, 38
Alabama Polytechnic Institute, 165
Altus, 139
Anderson, C. Alfred, 165
Anderson, Clarence, 78, 79, 80, 82, 83
Anglo-French Purchasing Commission, 11, 38
Archer, Lee, 177, 178
Armstrong, Louis, 170
Army Air Force Pursuit Board, 29
Arnold, Henry H., 25, 42, 43, 88
Atami, 90
Atwood, Lee, 14, 20
A6M, Mitsubishi, 33, 37, 38
AT-6, North American, 16, 27
A-26, Douglas, 129
A-36, North American, 25
Augusta, 139
Ayres, Frank, 92
Bader, Douglas, 142
Balfour, Paul, 21
Ballard, J.G., 8
Barber, Rex, 33
Barth, 132
Barton, Joe, 97, 98
Bassingbourn, 52
Battle of Britain, 121, 122, 124, 142
Battle of Britain, 136, 141
Battle of Britain Memorial Flight, 139
Beauvais, 140
Behling, Jr., George, 181, 183
Bendix Trophy Race, 129
Bellanca, 15
Bergstrom AFB, 101
Berlin, 46, 49, 51, 52, 58, 59, 65, 182
Berlin Express, 78
Berliner-Joyce, 14
Best Years of Our Lives, The, 129
Betty Jo, 108, 109
Bf 109, Messerschmitt, 23, 27, 38
Biak, 140
Blakeslee, Donald, 40, 43, 44, 45, 46, 50, 63, 64, 119, 122, 125, 127, 162, 163
Blaze of Noon, 130
Boeing Field, 85
Bong, Richard, 32
Bonn, 60
Boscombe Down, 22
Bougainville, 32
Breese, Vance, 21
Bretschneider, Klaus, 182
Buffalo, Brewster, 10
Bulldog, Bristol, 119, 120
Bungay, 52
Bunte, Allen, 56
B-17, Boeing, 35, 52, 55, 56, 67, 125, 126, 128, 138, 139, 179, 180
B-17 Preservation Ltd., 139
B-24, Consolidated, 35, 52, 55, 128, 139
B-25, North American, 16, 128, 129, 177
B-26, Douglas, 104, 106
B-26, Martin, 128, 152
B-29, Boeing, 84, 85, 87, 88, 89, 90, 91, 92, 93, 94, 95 99, 100, 116
B-36, Convair, 100
B-50, 100
BT-8, Seversky, 14
BT-9, North American, 15, 16
BT-13, Vultee, 137
Cal-Aero, 137
Cambridge, 119
Carpenter, Jesse, 62
Carswell AFB, 101
Casa 2.111, 142

Casarsa, 174
Cavalier 2000, 133, 134
Chamberlain, Neville, 9, 10
Chang Gin, 115
Chanute Field, 166
Chennault, Claire, 39
Chilton, Bob, 29, 31, 98
Chino, 136
Civilian Pilot Training Program, 164, 165
Churchill, Winston S., 10, 121
Clark, James, 58
Cleveland, 131
Clinton, 139
Coburn, Roscoe, 114
Cochran, Jacqueline, 130, 131
Coulson, R.L.S., 141
Combined Bombing Offensive, 7
Commemorative Air Force, 108
Concord, BAE, 7
Confederate Air Force, 108
Consolidated Aircraft, 15
Constellation, Lockheed, 7
Creil, 140
Crossley, Michael, 21
C-47, Douglas, 138
C-53, Douglas, 138
C-54, Douglas, 103, 104
Daladier, Edouard, 9
Davis, Benjamin O., Jr., 166, 167, 170, 171, 172, 177
Davis, Benjamin O., Sr., 166
Davis, Hubert, 138
Davis-Monthan AFB, 102
Dark Blue World, 139
Daymond, Gregory, 122
D-Day, 152, 153
DC-3, Douglas, 7
Debden, 43, 45, 46, 49, 50, 56, 65, 119, 121, 122, 123, 124
Deenethorpe, 52
Deere, Alan, 142
Derben, 180

De Vries, John, 143, 149, 150
Dieppe, raid, 121
Dodsworth, Red, 78
Doolittle, James, 133
Douglas Aircraft, 20
Douglas, Donald, 15
Dowding, H.C.T., 142
D0-217, Dornier, 47
Dregne, Irwin, 181
Dummer Lake, 182
Dunn, J.W., 181
Dunne, Charles, 176
Duxford, 137, 138
Eagle Squadrons, 121, 122, 123, 124
Eagle Squadron, 122
Eighth Air Force, 7, 8, 32, 42, 43, 44, 51, 53, 68, 70, 73, 162, 179, 181
83rd Fighter Squadron, 138
Ellison, James, 169
Empire of the Sun, 139
Elsberry, Joseph, 175, 176
England, John, 181
Farmer, James, 122
Fifteenth Air Force, 163, 171, 176, 177
15th Fighter Group, 85, 89, 90
52nd Fighter Group, 132
55th Fighter Group, 67
56th Fighter Group, 40, 43, 64
Fighter Collection, 137, 138
Fighter Rebuilders, 137
Fitzgerald, Ella, 170
Fitzgerald, F. Scott, 26
506th Fighter Group, 85, 93, 94
FJ-2, North American, 132
Fleet, Reuben, 15
Flying Legends, 138
Fokker, Anthony, 14, 19
Ford, Henry, 26
Framlingham, 50
Fritzlar, 140

Frey Packing Plant, 85
Fulda, 182
FG-1, Goodyear, 129, 130
F4F, Grumman, 138
F-5A, Lockheed, 60
F-6A, North American, 31
F6F, Grumman, 138
F8F, Grumman, 138
F-10, Fokker, 13
F-32, Fokker, 13
F-80, Lockheed, 104, 105
F-84, Republic, 101
F-86, North American, 102, 132, 135
F-94, Lockheed, 107
F-100, North American, 132
4th Fighter Group, 8, 43, 45, 50, 51, 57, 58, 63, 119, 125, 127, 162, 163
4th Fighter Squadron, 105
Fw 190, Focke-Wulf, 23, 47, 48, 64, 155, 156, 157, 158, 159, 174, 175, 177
Gabreski, Francis, 40
Galland, Adolf, 141, 142
Gasser, James, 181, 183
Gatwick, 23
Geiger, Bill, 123
General Aviation, 14, 19
General Motors, 13, 96
Gentile, Don, 47, 52, 53, 54, 55, 56, 65, 122
Gladiator, Gloster, 138
Godfrey, John, 45, 46, 47, 48, 49, 52, 53, 54, 55, 56, 65, 66
Goering, Hermann, 51
Goodson, James, 64
Goppingen, 140
Gover, Lee, 123
Great Marianas Turkey Shoot, 138
Grey, Stephen, 138
Guam, 88
Guilford, Bob, 135

Guthrie, Bill, 129
G4M, Mitsubishi, 33
Haedong, 110
Halesworth, 43, 44
Hall, Grover, 57, 119, 120, 126, 162
Halsey, Gilbert, 47
Hamburg, 89
Hamchang, 117
Hamhung, 115
Hangar Eleven Collection, 139
Hanna, Mark, 139
Hanna, Ray, 139
Hardwick Warbirds, 139
Harker, Ronald, 25, 42
Harvard, North American, 11, 16, 17, 27
Harvey, Gordon, 116, 117
Hawk, Curtiss, 10, 138
HA 1112, Hispano, 142
Heathrow, 10
Heiden, Art, 62
Heil, Charles, 91
Helseth, A.E., 110
Henlow, 141
Hesich-Lichtenau, 140
Hess, Dean, 110, 111
Heston, 10
He 111, Heinkel, 141
Hills, Hollis, 23
Hinton, Steve, 137, 138
Historic Aircraft Collection, 139
Historic Flying Limited, 139
Hitchcock, Thomas, Jr., 26, 42
Hitler, Adolf, 9, 52
Holm, Skip, 135
Hoover, Bob, 132
Horkey, Ed, 98
Hornbach, 11
Hudson, William, 103, 104
Hunter, Hawker, 7
Hurricane, Hawker, 10, 29, 38, 121, 138, 141

Ilfrey, Jack, 60, 61, 62, 63
Iwo Jima, 86, 89, 90, 91, 92
Itazuke AB, 102
Jenkins, Dittie, 181
JG300, 180, 182
JG301, 180
Johnson AAB, 143, 148, 149
Johnson, Kelly, 33, 34, 130
Johnson, Martin, 117
Johnson, Robert, 40
Julius Rosenwald Fund, 165
Ju-88, Junkers, 57, 59
Kaesong, 110
Kassel, 140
Kearney AFB, 100, 101
Kelso, Duane, 61, 62, 63
Kent, John, 142
Kepner, William, 44, 127, 162
Kettley, A.C., 119, 120, 121
Keystone Aircraft, 19
Kigye, 114
Kimble, Frederick von, 169
Kimbolton, 52
Kimpo AB, 102, 103, 104, 108
Kindelberger, J.H., 11, 14, 15, 16, 20, 24
Kingman, 139
King's Cliffe, 60, 63
Kirla, John, 181
Konantz, Walter, 67
Kozu, 90
Lacey, James, 142
Lackland AFB, 108, 109
Lacy, Clay, 135
Ladd AFB, 107
Lafayette Flying Corps, 26
Lambert, Mickie, 123
Lanphier, Thomas, 33
Latisana, 173
Last Seen in Combat Area, 179
Leiston, 68, 73, 179, 180
LeMay, Curtis E., 88, 93
Lend/Lease Act, 24

Louis, Joe, 170
L-4, Piper, 138, 140
L-5, Stinson, 140
LA-7, Lavochkin, 103, 104
Maastricht, 61
MaArthur, Douglas, 103, 111
Mace, Harvey, 36
Madrid, 142
Magdeburg, 60
Mahaddie, Hamish, 141, 142
Mahurin, Walker, 40
Malone, John, 135
Maloney, Ed. 137
Mantz, Paul, 128, 129, 130
Marchbanks, Jr., Vance, 171
Martlesham Heath, 49
Maxwell, Chester, 181
Maxwell Field, 161, 166, 168
McColpin, C.W., 122
McChord AFB, 101
McKain, W/hitey, 78, 79
McCullin, James, 177
Megura, Nicholas, 58, 59
Me-109, Messerschmitt, 47, 48, 53, 54, 58, 64, 67, 68, 81, 82, 141, 142, 177
Me-210, Messerschmitt, 47
Me-262, Messerschmitt, 138, 172
Memphis Belle, 139
Metcalf, George, 112
Miller, Glenn, 154
Missouri, USS, 94
Mitchell, Bill, 79, 82, 83
Molesworth, 52
Momyer, William, 171
Moran, Charles, 103
Munster, 125
Muritz Lake, 79
Murry, Jack, 114
Mussolini, Benito, 9
NA-16, North American, 14
NA-73, North American, 18, 20, 21
NA-97, North American, 25

NA-99, North American, 31
NACA, 108
Nagasaki, 94, 100
Nagoya, 91
Nimrod, Hawker, 138
Ninth Air Force, 8, 51, 127
99th Fighter Squadron, 163, 166, 167, 168, 171, 172, 173
Normandy, 153, 155
Nuremberg, 51
Ocean Venture, 22
Old Crow, 79
Old Flying Machine Co., 139
Old Yeller, 132
Olmsted, Merle, 68, 72, 179
100th Fighter Squadron, 171, 173
1000 Destroyed, 162
Ontario, 139
Osaka, 93
Oshkosh, 134
Overstreet, William, 77-83
P-38, Lockheed, 7, 24, 30-35, 37, 39, 60, 125, 129
P-39, Bell, 24, 35, 36, 37, 72, 78, 124, 128
P-40, Curtiss, 10, 11, 21, 30, 38, 39, 124, 128,
P-47, Republic, 7, 24, 29, 39, 40, 41, 43, 45, 72, 119, 124-128, 138
P-60, Curtiss, 29
P-61, Northrop, 30, 99
P-62, 29
P-63, Bell, 129
P-82, North American, 95-109
Packard Motor Car Co., 26
Packard-Merlin, 64, 70, 96, 134, 144
Palmdale, 130
Palm Springs Air Museum, 138
Parrish, Noel, 166, 169, 170
Pearl Harbor, 24, 30, 110, 122, 168
Personal Plane Services, 139
Peterson, Chesley, 122, 123

Piece of Cake, 142
Plane Sailing, 139
Planes of Fame, 137, 138
Podington, 52
Po'Hang, 112, 114, 117
Portal, Charles, 124
Pusan, 115
Pyongyang, 106, 116
Ramitelli Airfield, 171, 173, 174
Randolph Field, 171
Rau, Harold, 63
Raydon, 72, 75
Real Aeroplane Co., 139
Reconstruction Finance Corp, 139
Regina, Pete, 135
Reilly, Tom, 109
Rice, Ray, 98
Richards, Robert, 49, 52
Roberts, Leon, 163
Robinson, Derek, 142
Rockne, Knute, 14
Rolls-Royce Merlin, 10, 19, 25, 26, 45, 109
Roosevelt, Eleanor, 165
Roosevet, Franklin D., 24, 33, 42, 87, 88, 164
Ross, Mac, 163
Royal Navy Historic Flight, 139
Ruhland, 67
R-3350, Wright, 84, 85
Saffron Walden, 122
Saipan, 88
Sawyer, Harold, 175
Sebille, Louis, 117, 118
Schmued, Cristel, 135
Schmued, Edgar, 11-15, 18, 20, 21, 96, 989, 111, 113, 134
Schmued, Heinrich, 12
Schmued, Rolf, 135
Schmued, Sandra, 135
Seething, 52
Self, Henry, 11
71 Squadron, 121-123

77 Squadron, 115-117
Shuttleworth Collection, 139
66th Fighter Wing, 179
68th Fighter Squadron, 105, 106, 111
Smasher, The, 129
Snipes, Gil, 90, 91
Soplata, Walter, 109
Spencer, Chauncey, 164
Stalag Luft I, 132
Stearman, Boeing, 137
Steeple Morden, 45, 50, 162
Stillwater, 128
Stirling, Short, 141
Strobell, Robert, 75-77
Sudbury, 52
Taegu, 110, 112
Taejon, 112
Tagliamento, 173
Tapp, James, 92
Taylor, Frank, 131
21st Fighter Group, 85, 89
27th Fighter Escort Wing, 100, 101
27 Squadron, 123
33rd Fighter Group, 171
35th Fighter Group, 143
222nd Squadron, 123
301st Fighter Squadron, 171, 173, 174, 175
302nd Fighter Squadron, 171, 173, 174
332nd Fighter Group, 162, 171, 173, 174, 176
339th Fighter Group, 32, 106, 111
344th Bomb Group, 152, 162
347th Fighter Group, 32, 103
353rd Fighter Group, 75
357th Fighter Group, 36, 68, 71, 72, 77, 179, 180, 182
364th Fighter Squadron, 181
390th Bomb Group, 125
Thacker, Robert, 109
Therbeton, 180

Tiede, Ernest, 79
Tinian, 88, 95
Tobin, Eugene, 122
Tokyo, 88, 91,94
Tokyo Club, 86
Townsend, Peter, 142
Truman, Harry S., 24, 87, 102, 111, 164
Tuck, R. R. Stanford, 142
Tussey, Robert, 57
Twentieth Air Force, 88
Twilight Tear, 138
Tushino, 100
Tuskegee Airmen, 163, 165-169, 173, 176-178
TU-4, Tupolev, 100
Villacoublay, 157
Virgin, Ed, 98
Vraciu, Alex, 138
Waite, Larry, 98
Wanger, Walter, 123
Ward, Elmer, 135
White, Dale, 164
White, Sherman, 177
Winant, John, Jr., 126
Woodchurch Warbirds, 139
Woodrum, Henry, 162
Wormingford, 67
Wycombe Abbey, 8, 53
Yak-3, Yakovlev, 138
Yak-9, Yakovlev, 103, 111, 138
Yak-11, Yakovlev, 103
Yamamoto, Isoroku, 32, 33
Yankee Doodle Network, 154
Yanks Air Museum, 137
Yeager, Chuck, 135
Yongpo, 115
Yoxford, 180
Zemke, Hubert, 40, 43, 44, 51, 64
Zeuschel, Dave, 135